FEB   2012

CULTURES OF THE WORLD

Venezuela

Marshall Cavendish
Benchmark
New York

PICTURE CREDITS
Cover: © Peter Widmann / Imagebroker RM / glowimages.com
Corbis / Click Photos: 25, 27, 39, 44, 91 • Getty Images: 33, 78, 79, 86, 87, 88, 100, 111, 117, 121, 126, 130, 131 • Inmagine: 3, 9, 24, 26, 29, 30, 37, 45, 46, 58, 59, 61, 62, 70, 75, 77, 80, 81, 92, 95, 98, 101, 104, 116, 125, 128 • Lonely Planet Images: 82, 83, 85, 102, 119, 120, 122 • Marshall Cavendish International (Asia): 96, 103 • Photolibrary: 1, 5, 6, 8, 10, 11, 12, 13, 14, 15, 16, 17, 18, 19, 20, 22, 35, 41, 42, 47, 48, 49, 50, 52, 55, 63, 64, 65, 66, 67, 68, 71, 73, 84, 90, 94, 105, 106, 108, 112, 114, 127 • Reuters: 38, 40, 56, 118, 124

PRECEDING PAGE
Wild horses on the plains of the Andes Mountains.

Publisher (U.S.): Michelle Bisson
Writers: Jane Kohen Winter, Kitt Baguley
Editors: Deborah Grahame-Smith, Mindy Pang
Copyreader: Tara Tomczyk
Designers: Nancy Sabato, Lynn Chin
Cover picture researcher: Tracey Engel
Picture researcher: Joshua Ang

Marshall Cavendish Benchmark
99 White Plains Road
Tarrytown, NY 10591
Website: www.marshallcavendish.us

Library of Congress Cataloging-in-Publication Data
Winter, Jane Kohen, 1959-
 Venezuela / Jane Kohen Winter and Kitt Baguley.
  p. cm. — (Cultures of the world)
 Includes bibliographical references and index.
 Summary: "Provides comprehensive information on the geography, history, wildlife,
  governmental structure, economy, cultural diversity, peoples, religion, and culture
  of Venezuela"—Provided by publisher.
 ISBN 978-1-60870-803-1 (print) — ISBN 978-1-60870-799-7 (ebook)
 1. Venezuela—Juvenile literature. I. Baguley, Kitt. II. Title.

 F2308.5.W56 2013
 987—dc23   2011025226

Printed in Malaysia
7 6 5 4 3 2 1

CONTENTS

VENEZUELA TODAY

VENEZUELA IS A LAND OF SUPERLATIVES. IT IS THE WEALTHIEST nation in South America, thanks to its petroleum reserves. It has some of the world's oldest, most mysterious geologic formations; the world's highest waterfall; and some of the world's rarest, most unusual flowers and animals. Superlatives apply equally to the people of Venezuela. *Caraqueños* (kah-rah-KAIR-nyohs), citizens of the capital city—Caracas—are some of the most sophisticated South Americans. Simón Bolívar, one of South America's most revered heroes, who led several South American nations on the road to independence, was born in Caracas. The Venezuelan population also includes some of the toughest, most hardworking South Americans, the *llaneros* (yah-NAIR-rohs), cowboys of the grasslands. Every year, the *llaneros* battle extremely inhospitable weather conditions—floods in the wet season and drought in the dry season—to feed their cattle. Venezuela is also a country of stark contrasts. Driving into Caracas the first thing to be seen are the ramshackle brick shanty houses tumbling down the hillside and growing organically, one piling on top of another. Not far away are the impressive detached *quintas*, houses built to the wealthy owners' specifications, but always carefully walled and gated away from the public.

The llanos are one of the best places in the world to watch birds such as the heron, egret, and brilliant scarlet ibis (*above*), which is found only in northern South America.

As you drive into the city, the crush of traffic and the modern cityscape of tall office buildings and apartments are clear, along with the occasional bloated dog carcass. Caracas seemed to be a busy, fairly dirty, youthful, and vibrant city. It has been said that Caracas is a city that is hard to fall in love with, but it is soon obvious there is plenty to do: whether it is going to the cinema to watch dubbed Hollywood films, going to a jazz concert at the Teatro Teresa Carreño, a gig with a rising Venezuelan pop star at a country club, or a jazz club, or just enjoying the beaches near the city.

It is easy to become accustomed to the love of food, especially meat, including barbecues (*parilla*), whiskey and dancing at private parties, and the eagerness for the weekend and for any chance to take more days off.

Notable differences include the way a scratch game of soccer takes forever to get started, or waiting for a date to turn up takes hours, or the impossibility of getting reliable information or doing any business at all over the phone and the need to have more than one face-to-face meeting. Then there is to the mix of modern and old, with beautiful young people in the latest European or U.S. fashions hurrying along with men in the traditional Venezuelan dress *liqui-liquis* and straw hats.

The occasional flash of natural beauty amid the city reminds visitors that they are in a country rich with wildlife. There might be a pair of gargantuan iguanas in the branches of a small tree overlooking the highway, or parrots bursting over an apartment block with a flash of green and raucous cries, or vultures circling slowly overhead in search of carrion.

There is the kindness shown to strangers and the warmth of hospitality, but then there is also the indifference to ambulances struggling through the traffic. More worrying still is the gun crime and a natural mistrust of the heavily armed police or lighter-armed army. The frenetic energy of the traffic and pressures of trying to get around the city to do business stands in contrast to the relatively relaxed nature of most work and people's lack of interest in public service. In a bank, girls chat and do their nails while customers wait for service. Cities are characterized by the ancient and unlovely cars and the endless workshops that keep them going.

In contrast to the cities, the calm of the countryside and small towns and villages is noticeable. In the villages, chickens and dogs roam freely; there is a sense of tranquillity and awareness of the natural world. There is a quiet and stillness that allows you to appreciate the scents of trees and plants and the sounds of bird calls with the odd intrusion of man-made sounds, such as the clanking of pots. People do nothing for hours on end, awaiting the next meal or the next thing to happen.

The physical extremes of Venezuela offer much of interest, from the humidity of the Amazon rain forests and the tea-brown Orinoco, teeming with ants and anacondas and red howler monkeys. The Amerindians, traditionally dressed or in Disney T-shirts, live a rural life much the same as anyone else's, or an unenviable urban existence or, rarely, a traditional lifestyle that excites the imagination of Westerners. There is a dramatic plane flight over the Andes to Merida and over small towns with houses painted in pastels with bright-white churches among them. The mountain landscape (*paramo*) is misty, dotted with the semi-cactus succulent squashy *frailejones*. Elsewhere Venezuela boasts the surprising sand dunes of Coro and the architecture of the ancient capital, the tourist-trap beaches of Puerto La Cruz, Margarita, and Los Roques with good restaurants everywhere. The *tepuis*, rainbows, and falls of Roraima, La Gran Sabana, and the endless, merciless plains of Los Llanos, dusty and intensely beautiful in the sunset. The cloud forest in Monagas, haunting and transcendental, a place of quiet stasis, closer to Nirvana than Limbo.

Venezuela can seem like an earthly paradise and used to be one of the most prosperous countries in Latin America. However, life has changed

A woman in the traditional Venezuelan outfit.

dramatically for Venezuelans since the charismatic populist Hugo Chávez came to power in 1999. His time as president has changed the fortunes of millions of people, some for the better, some for the worse. His programs have reduced poverty by 30 percent between 1995 and 2005. He has implemented free health care, subsidized food for the poor, and has redistributed land to aid small-scale farmers.

The country is divided between his supporters, known as Chavistas, and his opponents, and opinions about Chávez are similarly divided across the world. Chávez sees himself as a modern-day Bolívar, continuing the work of the 19th-century statesman who led the fight for Latin America's independence from Spain and advocated the creation of a league of Latin American states. Chávez has reached out to socialist and communist countries in South America, the Caribbean, and further abroad to spread his Bolivarian philosophy.

The effects of this approach can be clearly seen in Venezuela today. There are now Cubans in the health and security services: more than 15,000 Haitians, many working as street vendors; more than 50,000 Chinese immigrants, many of whom are shopkeepers; and thousands of workers from Arab countries, such as Syria, Jordan, and Lebanon. There are also more than 4 million Colombians living in Venezuela, as well as thousands more immigrants from other regional neighbors.

Hundreds of thousands of educated Venezuelans have left the country to find work and new homes in the United States. They are known as *balseros de aire*, or "rafters of the air," after the Cubans who fled to the United States when Fidel Castro came to power. Rather than using rafts, they have flown away, showing that they had enough wealth and opportunity to escape in comfort. Many professional people, including doctors, engineers, scientists, and businesspeople, have left. These include thousands of Jews, who are worried that the government's policies are anti-Semitic.

Other current concerns for Venezuelans include the environment, most urgently the dangers from flooding that affects mainly the poorer hillside ranchos. Most recently, in 2010, landslides destroyed the homes of many thousands of people and Chávez issued decrees to enable displaced people to occupy unused houses. Most controversially many buildings in Chacao, a fairly prosperous neighborhood of Caracas, were taken over by those who had been made homeless. The landslides also damaged roads and other infrastructure, and the cost of repairs added to the burdens of a struggling economy. Conversely droughts in the same year caused blackouts across the country because the Guri dam could not produce electricity. This single dam provides 73 percent of Venezuela's electricity.

A group of happy local children playing in the water with some old inner tube floats in Santa Fe.

In Venezuela's heyday, when its oil-rich economy was booming, it grew culturally closer to the United States. Shopping trips to Miami were common for the wealthy middle and upper classes. American clothes and sports became more and more popular. Venezuelans often studied English in the United States, or in language schools or international schools across the country. Now, as Chávez's government aims to create closer ties with other Latin countries, it is more hostile to the United States and other Western countries.

This means that the Venezuelan government does not offer a friendly face to the interested Western observer. All government-controlled media outlets are strong voices for Chávez's agenda and all now give information in Spanish alone. Many websites that were available in English have been made Spanish only. There is often strong anti-Chávez sentiment in the international media, and this is fueled by rising crime, fears of government interference in the Venezuelan media to restrict freedom of speech, and interference in the internal affairs of other countries in the region, as well as allegations of corruption and political oppression. Travelers are also warned that levels of street crime are high and that kidnappings and carjackings are frequent. There is frequent violence associated with drug-trafficking and rebel groups near the Colombian border and danger from mass demonstrations and marches. Despite this, Venezuela attracts more than 7 million visitors a year, especially to the major tourist destinations such as Margarita Island.

Cultures of the World: Venezuela explores the history, government, economy, environment, people, faiths, festivals, food, and lifestyles of this remarkable country in South America.

GEOGRAPHY

An aerial view of the Orinoco River surrounded by tropical rain forests.

1

T HE SEVENTH-LARGEST COUNTRY in South America, Venezuela lies in the north of the continent. With a total area of 352,144 square miles (912,050 square kilometers), Venezuela is slightly more than twice the size of California, about four times the size of Great Britain, around 28 times the size of Holland, yet only one-tenth the size of Brazil.

The world's longest continental mountain range, the Andes, stretches through many South American countries, including Venezuela.

There are two sides to Venezuela. It is no coincidence that Venezuela's cities are located along the coast, which has long been the key to Venezuela's wealth. The rest of the country is referred to as *El Interior*—"the Interior"—which makes it seem unknown and mysterious. *El Interior* is where the cultural wealth of the preceding centuries can be found. It is far less influenced by the United States and international Latin culture than the cities are.

Venezuela's coastline stretches 1,740 miles (2,800 km) and abuts both the Caribbean Sea and the Atlantic Ocean. Half of the country is covered by forests and beaches; the other half consists of mountains, plains, deserts, and grasslands. Venezuelan land can be divided into four distinct geographical regions: the Andean Highlands, the Maracaibo basin, the llanos, and the Guiana Highlands.

THE ANDEAN HIGHLANDS

The Andean Highlands lie in the west and along the coast. They include the Andean mountain range within the Venezuelan border. Although these highlands represent only 12 percent of Venezuela's land area, they are home to 66 percent of the national population and most of the major cities. The capital city, Caracas, is in this region. Due to its pleasant climate, Caracas has been called "Los Angeles without the smog." It is one of the world's most sophisticated cities, with a skyline of high-rise office and apartment buildings and a modern French-designed subway system. Yet the capital is as poor as it is wealthy: thousands of *caraqueños* live in ranchos, or makeshift shacks, on the fringes of the city.

Mount Kukenan in the Canaima National Park is one example of a *tepui*, or "house of the gods," a term describing mountains with a flat top.

THE MARACAIBO BASIN

The second major geographical region, the Maracaibo basin, lies in the northwest of the country. This region contains Lake Maracaibo, the largest lake in South America. This shallow freshwater lake is 75 miles (121 km) long and 100 miles (161 km) wide. At the northern tip, where the lake opens into the Caribbean Sea, lies the port of Maracaibo. In the early part of the 20th century, the most important oil wells in Venezuela were discovered in Lake Maracaibo. At present the lake is dotted with thousands of oil derricks that extract millions of barrels of oil each year. With a population of more than 2 million, the city of Maracaibo is the second-largest city in Venezuela. It is accessible via the 5-mile-long (8-km-long) General Raphael Urdaneta Bridge, the longest pre-stressed concrete bridge in the world.

THE LLANOS

The llanos, or plains, are located in the central part of the country. They account for nearly one-third of Venezuelan land, yet they are home to only 9 percent of the population. This low population density is due to the extremely harsh landscape and climate. The land is flat and almost treeless, and the seasons range from scorching hot to soaking wet. Five million heads of cattle live in the llanos. The herds are driven by the cowboys, or *llaneros*, to wetter areas during the dry season and to drier areas during the wet season.

An aerial view of the llanos of Venezuela and flight of birds.

The Guiana Highlands have been used as a setting in a famous piece of literature. Sir Arthur Conan Doyle's The Lost World, *originally published in 1912, is a fantasy-adventure tale about an expedition by four English adventurers to a remote region in Venezuela, where 20-foot (6.1-meter) pterodactyls, gigantic three-toed, black-skinned dinosaurs, and apemen still roamed.*

Prehistoric creatures do not, of course, exist in the Guiana Highlands. But the Guiana Highlands have in fact been a largely unexplored place, due to the unfriendly terrain.

"It's the grandest, richest, most wonderful bit of earth upon this planet. . . . Why shouldn't somethin' new and wonderful lie in such a country? And why shouldn't we be the men to find out?" asks a character from The Lost World. *Modern scientists and explorers are perhaps asking themselves the same question. Apart from scattered groups of Indians, no one inhabits the Guiana Highlands. However, industry has found its way into the region to exploit bauxite, iron ore, and gold deposits and to generate hydroelectric power. Much of the mining in the region is illegal and the rest is under-regulated, causing unknown environmental damage.*

THE GUIANA HIGHLANDS

Located in the south and east of Venezuela, the Guiana Highlands account for almost half the nation's land, yet are almost completely uninhabited. These highlands consist mainly of ancient, vast sandstone formations called *tepuis* (teh-POO-ees), or tablelands. The *tepuis* can reach as high as 6,000 feet (1,829 meters) and have been eroded at the base. Because many of the *tepuis* in this region are very steep and virtually unscalable, much of the Guiana Highlands remain unexplored.

The Guiana Highlands also contain the world's highest waterfall, Angel Falls, first spotted by pilot James Angel in 1935 while he was searching for gold. At 3,212 feet (979 m), the falls are more than 15 times taller than Niagara Falls, or twice the height of New York's Empire State Building. Strangely enough Angel Falls does not flow over a cliff. The water actually accumulates underground and erupts through cracks in the mountain.

The largest city in the Guiana Highlands is Ciudad Guayana, with 746,500 inhabitants. Guayana is the fifth-largest city in Venezuela and a hub for heavy industry.

The world's highest waterfall, Angel Falls, is located at the edge of the Auyantepui mountain in Canaima National Park.

THE ISLANDS

Venezuelan territory includes 72 islands in the Caribbean Sea. Margarita Island, known for its beaches and colonial architecture, is a favorite resort for Venezuelans and tourists.

THE GREAT ORINOCO

Columbus was the first known explorer to see the mouth of the Orinoco River. This river, with its 436 tributaries, is the third-longest river in South America and the eighth-longest in the world. It flows 1,370 miles (2,205 km) from the Guiana Highlands to the Atlantic Ocean. On the way the Orinoco splits into 100 separate channels, and at the end of the journey, the channels rush into the Atlantic Ocean with such great force that there is fresh water for miles out to sea.

At one point the Orinoco River connects with the great Amazon River through a waterway called the Casiquiare Canal. It is said that together the Orinoco and the Amazon form the greatest river system in the world. They

The Los Roques archipelago of islands is a federal dependency of Venezuela.

carry more water and drain a larger area than both the Missouri—Mississippi system and the Nile. In fact more than a third of South America—an area of approximately 2.5 million square miles (6.5 million square km)—is dominated by the Orinoco—Amazon river system. The Orinoco also provides important communication links with the interior of Venezuela and hydroelectric power for a large part of the country.

A view of Raudales Atures, the rapids that block the Orinoco River navigation in Puerto Ayacucho.

CLIMATE

Although Venezuela lies completely within the tropical zone, temperatures vary from region to region, depending on elevation and prevailing winds. Lowland areas remain warm throughout the year. The country's highest average annual temperature of 83°F (28°C) occurs in the central part of the llanos and the north of the Maracaibo basin. The weather gets much cooler at higher altitudes, and snow covers the highest Andean peaks all year-round.

The country basically has three temperature zones. The "hot land" is humid, with average daily temperatures exceeding 75°F (24°C) but rarely topping 95°F (35°C). In the "temperate land," average daily temperatures range from 50 to 80°F (10 to 27°C). In the "cold land," temperatures fall below 65°F (18°C) during the day and reach the freezing point at night.

Cactus in the central Venezuelan desert.

In the wet months, May to October, the llanos and forests become swampy and green, but in the dry season, these areas become parched and brown. Rainfall averages less than 20 inches (51 centimeters) on the mountainous coast. The Orinoco delta and the south of the Maracaibo basin receive up to 80 inches (203 cm) of rainfall annually. The plateaus of the Guiana Highlands receive moderate rainfall. Caracas gets about 32 inches (81 cm) a year, as much as the city of Chicago gets.

FLORA

Venezuela has more plant species than the United States and Canada have together. On mountain slopes below 3,000 feet (914.4 m), tropical forests with dense shrubbery are most common. Scrubby woodland and dense forest filled with exotic orchids—such as the Venezuelan national flower, the deep pink cattleya mossiae—cover slopes between 3,000 and 6,000 feet (914.4 and 1,828.8 m). Above 6,000 feet vegetation is sparse. Grasses and herbaceous plants are most common. In the alpine regions, from 10,000 to 15,000 feet (3,048 to 4,572 m), there is little plant life. The landscape here consists of high pastures freckled with the yellow flowering *frailejón* (fray-lay-HON) tree. The leaves of this tree resemble rabbits' ears and have been used as mattress stuffing.

In the Maracaibo region, high humidity and heavy rainfall support lush tropical forests. Near the Caribbean Sea, however, the air is drier, and desert plants are more common.

The llanos are Venezuela's natural pasture, thanks to light soils and alternating wet and dry seasons. The plains contain more flora than the African grasslands. To the east, in the Orinoco delta, the land is swampy and full of mangrove thickets. Most of the Guiana Highlands are covered with

Capybaras running freely in the llanos of Venezuela.

rough natural grass and semi-deciduous tropical forest tangled with vines and parasitic growth. Unusual plant and animal species and rare orchids populate the 1.8-billion-year-old Mount Roraima, the tallest of the region's *tepuis*, rising 9,219 feet (2,810 m) above sea level.

FAUNA

The Andean Highlands are home to monkeys, bears, deer, wild pigs, otters, sloths, anteaters, foxes, opossums, armadillos, rodents, and big cats such as jaguars, ocelots, and pumas.

The lowlands of the *llanos* compare with the African continent in terms of the variety of wildlife. Many animal species that are threatened elsewhere have survived in the Andean Highlands because of the absence of a large human population.

Besides the 5 million cattle that roam the llanos, some of the world's most unusual animals make their home in this central region of Venezuela. The capybara, which lives in the swampy areas, has the distinction of being the world's largest rodent. It can weigh up to 100 pounds (45.4 kilograms) and looks more like a friendly beaver or otter than a giant rat. The capybara has partially webbed toes, no tail, and a cleft palate. It eats only plants and communicates by making a low grunting noise.

The Orinoco River contains a large variety of fish, including a species of catfish that can weigh up to 300 pounds (136 kg). Rare river mammals such as the dolphin and sea cow or manatee are also found in the fresh waters of the Orinoco.

The orchid commonly called the green-lipped cycnoches chlorochilon can carry 3.7 million seeds in a single pod. This is to guarantee propagation, since many of the seeds die before they germinate.

The Orinoco dolphin has small eyes, pink skin, a long beak, and a humped back. Unlike other freshwater dolphins, Orinoco dolphins live in schools of 12 to 20 and show signs of group loyalty. A smaller species that grows to only 5 to 6 feet (1.5 to 1.8 m) in length is considered sacred by some local Indians. This species has the "smiling" face commonly associated with the ocean-bound bottle-nosed dolphin.

The Orinoco crocodile also makes its home in the llanos. The German naturalist Alexander von Humboldt, exploring the Orinoco in the early 1800s, reported seeing crocodiles that measured up to 24 feet (7.3 m) in length. Today a male Orinoco crocodile may grow up to 16.4 feet (5 m). Between 1920 and 1940 almost 2 million Orinoco crocodiles were killed for their hides, and they have become one of the most endangered animal species in the world. Despite serious conservation efforts and the collapse of trade in crocodile hides, only 250 to 1,500 of these reptiles are left in Venezuela and Colombia.

Every new exploration into the 7.4 million acres (2.99467 hectares) of jungle in the Guiana Highlands uncovers new animal species never before documented. The harsh terrain and climate have insulated the area from human activity and forced plants and animals indigenous to the region to

The tiny but long-legged burrowing owls are found in the open landscapes of Venezuela.

develop interesting survival traits and tactics. For example one expedition discovered a species of toad with feet specially adapted for climbing rocky cliffs and a catfish with a full beard used to attract mates.

In the famous Guácharo Cave in northeast Venezuela lives the oilbird, or *guácharo* (goo-AH-chah-roh), which has been an object of curiosity since 1799 when Humboldt told the scientific world of its existence. Ten thousand oilbirds live in the Guácharo Cave, within the boundaries of a 34,000-acre (13.7593-ha) reserve.

Oilbirds have reddish-brown feathers. They measure from 12 to 18 inches (30 to 46 cm) in length and have a wing span of more than 3 feet (0.9 m). Oilbirds are nocturnal, as bats are. During the day oilbirds sleep crowded together in the black Guácharo Cave. At dusk they fly out to find food—the oily nut of the palm tree—using echolocation. Most of their waking hours are spent in flight.

The oilbird got its name in the early 1800s when it was hunted by Indians and missionaries for its fat, which was made into lamp oil. Today it is illegal to kill an oilbird.

INTERNET LINKS

www.atozkidsstuff.com/ven.html

This site provides general information on Venezuela, with an emphasis on geography.

www.venzuelatuya.com/geografia/indexeng.htm

This website provides plenty of information about Venezuela, with interesting visual presentations.

www.dosmanosnederland.com/en/destinations/venezuela/geography-environment.php

This is a website for travelers, with some very useful information on Venezuela.

HISTORY

A statue of Simón Bolívar, the Liberator, at the Independence Monument in Caracas.

BOLIVAR

2

THE SEARCH FOR GOLD SHAPED Venezuela's early history, although gold is not the country's main natural resource. According to myth, a "gilded man," or "El Dorado," made his kingdom in northern South America. This Indian chief was supposed to have been so wealthy that he went about dusted in gold. Every night he washed the gold dust off, and every morning he reapplied it.

With dreams of possessing the kingdom of El Dorado, European explorers traveled to present-day Venezuela in the last years of the 15th century. When Christopher Columbus reached the coast in the 1490s, he wrote to his king and queen to claim the land for Spain and to tell of the Indians he had seen with pearls around their necks and arms.

In 1499 Spanish explorer Alfonso de Ojeda made a memorable expedition to the northern part of Venezuela. Seeing Indian huts built on stilts in Lake Maracaibo, Ojeda and his mapmaker—Amerigo Vespucci, after whom America was named—were reminded of the canals of Venice, so they named the country "Little Venice," or Venezuela.

THE FIRST INHABITANTS

Like the rest of the Americas Venezuela was originally inhabited by Indians, who had made their way across the Bering Strait from Asia during the Ice Age. Between 20,000 and 10,000 B.C., South America was

Venezuela's history is a source of great national pride. A statue of the Liberator of South America, Simón Bolívar, stands in almost every town square across the nation. The names of many of his fellow heroes of independence adorn statues and monuments, states, street names, and universities across Venezuela. The power they still hold shows in the "Bolivarian" label that accompanies so many of the government's innovations.

Indian huts, or old *palafitos*, on stilts on the Laguna De Sinamaica in Zulia.

populated by hunters who fed on mastodons and giant sloths. By 1000 B.C. these hunters, the peaceful Arawak, had become farmers. They were driven from the land by the warlike Carib.

When Columbus first saw the Indians of Venezuela in October 1492, he described them as being "of tanned color . . . neither black nor white"; well-built, with "no belly"; and having a broad forehead, straight legs, and black hair that was "straight and coarse like horsehair."

The Venezuelan Indians were accomplished farmers, great artisans, and rich in religious ritual, but they were not as highly organized as the Aztecs, Incas, or Mayas. Although they fought the Spanish conquistadores with great spirit, they were overcome.

THE SPANISH CONQUEST

In 1509 the first European settlement in all of South America was founded on the Venezuelan island of Cubagua. The settlers had come in search of pearls, but by 1550 the pearl beds were dry and the island was abandoned. Around 1520 the first permanent Spanish settlement was founded at Cumaná, on the northeastern coast of Venezuela.

The town of Coro, founded in 1527, is significant in Venezuela's history. To pay his debts Charles I of Spain mortgaged the town to the German banking house of Wesler. In search of El Dorado, the Weslers made expeditions into the Venezuelan interior, looting the country and killing many indigenous inhabitants, yet finding no gold. In 1546 Spain terminated its agreement with the Germans and, giving up the search for gold, opted to develop Venezuela agriculturally.

By the end of the 16th century, 20 towns had been established. Many of the Indians were forced to become slaves on the sugar and coffee haciendas, or plantations, of the Spanish settlers. Millions of slaves died, and landowners imported African slaves from the Caribbean islands to work in the fields. Although South America had nearly 50 million indigenous Indians in the 15th century, only 2 million survived the conquest. Most of the remaining Indians, who lived in the llanos and Maracaibo regions, were colonized by the Dominican, Jesuit, Franciscan, and Augustinian missionaries from Spain who, by the early 1700s, had spread Christianity to remote parts of the country.

A 1565 artist's rendition of Venezuelan Indians fighting against the Spaniards.

The male Spanish settlers, called *peninsulars* (pay-nihn-SOO-lars), held powerful positions in the colonies. They eventually married indigenous women, producing mestizos, children of Spanish and Indian parentage. Criollos, or Creoles, were people of Spanish heritage born in Venezuela. They held prominent positions at the local level and resented the dominant class of *peninsulars*. The criollos also intermarried. People of African origin, who were brought over as slaves, were considered the lowest class.

THE INDEPENDENCE MOVEMENT

Like the U.S. independence movement the Venezuelan movement had its roots in the desire of Venezuelans to trade freely with other nations.

In 1728 the Real Compañia Guipuzcoana de Caracas was established, giving the Basques from Spain exclusive rights to import goods into Venezuela. In 1785, however, because of local jealousy and opposition to the monopoly of foreign trade by the Europeans, the company was dismantled and free trade was granted, but only within the Spanish Empire.

SIMÓN BOLÍVAR, THE LIBERATOR

Simón Bolívar is Venezuela's most revered citizen. Born in Caracas to wealthy criollo parents in 1783, Bolívar traveled to Europe in 1799 and 1803. In France he was influenced by the revolutionary spirit of the Parisians, who inspired his dream of independence for Venezuela.

Bolívar was a thin, small man, with a lean face and vibrant black eyes. A good horseman and swimmer, he had an amazing amount of energy. His soldiers were devoted to him, and the British Romantic poet, Lord Byron, was so enamored of him that he named his boat Bolivar and actually made plans to move to Venezuela with his daughter.

Bolívar was a brilliant orator, and his speeches are still read and respected today. In 1812, when Caracas was destroyed by an earthquake, he said, "If Nature opposes our designs, we shall fight against her and make her obey." Bolívar died in 1830 at the age of 47.

In 1797 Great Britain occupied the island of Trinidad for the purpose of selling goods illegally to Venezuela. To foil British attempts, Spain decided to allow free trade among all nations. However, in 1802, the Spaniards changed their minds and decided once again to limit free trade. Led by *caraqueño* Francisco de Miranda, many angry Venezuelans revolted, beginning the independence movement.

This initial foray into self-rule was not successful, however, and Miranda was exiled. He returned in 1810 and, the following year, was proclaimed dictator of Venezuela. The country then had a population of about 700,000, 60 percent of African heritage. Miranda's dictatorship was short-lived, however. By 1812 he was captured by forces still in favor of Spanish rule.

Simón Bolívar, also a *caraqueño* and Miranda's former aide, invaded Venezuela in 1813, reestablished the republic, appointing himself as

"I will never allow my hands to be idle or my soul to rest until I have broken the shackles which chain us to Spain."
—Simón Bolívar, as a student in Europe

dictator, and gained the title of Liberator. Unfortunately the new republic was destroyed again in 1814 by a group of plains cowboys, or *llaneros*, who still had royalist leanings. Bolívar was forced into exile but returned in 1817 to establish the third republic.

In 1819 Bolívar devised a grand scheme to bring what are now Venezuela, Ecuador, and Colombia together to form one independent state: Gran Colombia. It was not until 1821, however, that Bolívar accomplished his scheme by defeating the Spanish at Carabobo.

Miranda and Bolívar lead their followers in the signing of the Declaration of Independence for Venezuela against Spanish rule on July 5, 1811.

In 1830 Venezuela seceded from Gran Colombia and became truly independent. José Antonio Páez, who had expelled the last Spanish garrison in 1823, was named president.

THE TURBULENT ROAD TO DEMOCRACY

From 1908 to 1935 Venezuela was dominated by a fierce dictator. With the army and police under his control, General Juan Vicente Gómez ruled by repression and terror. The years between 1936 and 1948 enjoyed democratic rule and the election to the presidency of the country's most famous novelist, Rómulo Gallegos. Political unrest followed, and from 1950 to 1958, Venezuela fell under the control of another dictator, General Marcos Pérez Jiménez. His tenure was marked by corruption and brutal suppression of the opposition, though he did make contributions, building roads and housing projects in Caracas.

It was not until 1958 that Rómulo Betancourt and his democratic party, Acción Democrática (AD), brought lasting democracy to Venezuela. Betancourt is famous for his philosophy of "sowing the oil," or using petroleum profits for the benefit of the people. Betancourt tackled social problems such as illiteracy, poor living conditions and education facilities, and a high infant mortality rate.

Carlos Andrés Pérez was elected president in 1974 and again in 1989. He nationalized the petroleum industry and launched ambitious programs in education and agriculture. In foreign relations Venezuela, through Pérez, became an important advocate of human rights and economic independence. Pérez survived two military coup attempts before being tried in 1993 on charges of misappropriating $17 million in government funds; he was suspended permanently from the presidency.

In 1993 Rafael Caldera led his Convergencia coalition party to election victory, breaking the decades-long hold on power of AD and the Social Christian Party (COPEI). In 1994 President Caldera responded to a financial crisis involving the collapse of several banks by suspending civil liberties, which were restored in 1995, except in turbulent border zones. The 1995 municipal and regional elections saw a voter turnout of only 40 percent and the decline of Caldera's popularity.

In the 1998 elections Hugo Chávez Frías of the Fifth Republic Movement (MVR) rode to power on a wave of popular support. He appealed to the working classes by promising improved workers' rights, constitutional changes, and an anti-corruption drive. In 1999 a National Constituent Assembly (ANC) replaced the senate and congress. Chávez supporters won 90 percent of the 131 seats. The ANC proposed a new constitution, approved by more than 70 percent of voters. Under this constitution the country was renamed the "Bolivarian Republic of Venezuela." In the same year the north of Venezuela was devastated by floods and landslides. Tens of thousands were killed and many more lost their homes. In the 2000 elections Chávez beat former ally Francisco Arias Cardenas, but his Patriotic Pole alliance won 60 percent of the National Constituent Assembly seats, not quite enough to form a majority. There was also an unsuccessful plot to assassinate Chávez in the same year.

In 2002 more than 150,000 people held a rally to protest oil reforms and to support a general strike. More than 10 people died and 110 were injured in clashes with the National Guard. Chávez was taken into military custody and his resignation was announced. Pedro Carmona was named as head of the transitional government. Within two days the transitional government collapsed and Chávez returned to power. Strikes in December caused national oil shortages.

In 2003 the opposition handed in a petition with 3.4 million signatures to demand a referendum on Chávez's presidency. The following year Chávez won the referendum as voters asked him to see out the two and a half years left of his current term. Elections in 2006 brought Chávez back into power for another four-year term as he won 63 percent of the vote.

In a 2007 referendum Chávez suffered his first major democratic setback as Venezuelans voted against extending the speed and size of his reforms. Venezuelans voted in a referendum to abolish term limits in 2009, allowing Chávez to run for re-election again in 2012. His powers were extended in 2010 to deal with disastrous floods. Those who had lost their homes were entitled to settle on "unoccupied land."

Remains of a Spanish fortress in the Paraguana Peninsula. Evidence of the Spanish conquest is found in Venezuela's forts and religious institutions.

INTERNET LINKS

http://news.bbc.co.uk/1/hi/world/americas/country_profiles/1229348.stm

This BBC News site provides a detailed look at Venezuela's history in a time line.

www.venezuelatuya.com/historia/resum1eng.htm

Called Venezuela Tuya, this site is well presented and provides easy-to-read pages on Venezuelan history.

www.historyorb.com/countries/venezuela

This site provides a list of dates and fast facts about Venezuela, many of which will not be found elsewhere.

www.history.com/topics/hugo-chavez

This website from the History Channel provides concise political biographies of Hugo Chávez and other notable Venezuelan figures.

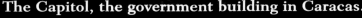

GOVERNMENT

The Capitol, the government building in Caracas.

3

T HE REPUBLIC OF VENEZUELA is one of Latin America's oldest functioning democracies. It is made up of 23 states, the Federal District of Caracas, and a Federal Dependency consisting of 311 islands and keys organized into 11 federally controlled groups. In 1985 the states were subdivided into 156 districts and 613 municipalities.

NATIONAL GOVERNMENT

The Venezuelan government can be divided into five branches: the executive, legislative, judicial, citizens, and electoral.

The executive branch consists of a cabinet of ministers headed by the president, who is both chief of state and head of government. The president is elected for a six-year term and may be re-elected for additional terms without limit. He or she works in conjunction with the Congress—the legislative branch—to determine the size and composition of the cabinet. The president also appoints the vice president, subject to approval by the Congress. The legislative branch is composed of 165 representatives who are elected to a five-year term and can be re-elected without limit.

Legislation can be initiated by the executive branch, the legislative branch (either a committee of the National Assembly or three members of the latter), the judicial branch, the citizen branch or a public petition

Hugo Chávez is working to extend his Bolivarian revolution beyond Venezuela. Chávez has combined Simón Bolívar's ideal of a political union of South America, extended it to the Caribbean, and blended in aspects of modern life. The Bolivarian Alliance for the Peoples of Our America (*Alianza Bolivariana para los Pueblos de Nuestra América*, or ALBA) aligns the region's nations socially, politically, and economically. It boasts its own regional currency, named the Sucre (after the revolutionary hero José Antonio de Sucre).

signed by no fewer than 0.1 percent of registered voters. The president can ask the National Assembly to reconsider portions of laws, but can then be overridden by a simple majority of the Assembly.

Other presidential duties include making and ratifying international treaties, conventions, and agreements; directing foreign affairs; commanding the armed forces; calling a state of emergency when necessary; ordering the suspension of constitutional guarantees when necessary; and introducing and defending bills before the Congress.

Under the 1999 constitution the former bicameral Congress, consisting of a senate and chamber of deputies, was replaced by a single-chamber Congress, the National Assembly. Members of the National Assembly are elected by popular vote to serve five-year terms; a few seats are reserved for representatives of indigenous Venezuelans.

The National Assembly has the power to approve, amend, or reject legislation proposed by the executive branch. The president can, however, veto bills passed by the National Assembly or order the Congress to reconsider amendments made to proposed legislation.

The president can also dissolve the National Assembly in times of crisis or if the National Assembly twice rejects the presidential choice for vice president. However, the National Assembly can, with a two-thirds majority, override the president's veto.

The judicial branch of the Venezuelan government consists of the Supreme Court of Justice. The National Assembly elects the 18 members of the Supreme Court for 12-year terms. Supreme Court justices serve only one term.

The Supreme Court of Justice holds ultimate judicial power; it is the highest court in the land, and its decisions cannot be appealed. It can declare a law or an act of the president unconstitutional, and it can determine whether the president and members of the National Assembly can be put on trial.

Each state has its own Supreme Court as well as lower courts. The judicial council selects judges for the lower civilian courts.

A council consisting of the public prosecutor, general accountant, and defender of the people (a national ombudsman) investigates acts against the public's interest and works to ensure the legal use of public funds.

Represented by the attorney general, the ombudsman (or *Defensor del Pueblo*) and controller general, the citizens power branch protects the rights of the Venezuelan people and guards against violations of the constitution.

Represented by the National Electoral Council, the electoral power branch independently organizes, executes, and monitors elections in Venezuela.

VOTING

Voting in presidential elections is noncompulsory for all Venezuelans over the age of 18. Elections are organized and supervised by the National Electoral Council (CNE), which consists of five members elected by the National Assembly for a seven-year term.

The constitution guarantees the freedom to form political parties. A party must obtain 1 percent of the national vote in order to retain its legal status. The major parties include A New Time, or UNT; Brave People's Alliance, or ABP; Communist Party of Venezuela, or PCV; Fatherland for All, or PPT; For Social Democracy, or PODEMOS; Justice First; The Radical Cause; United Socialist Party of Venezuela, or PSUV (the party of Hugo Chávez); Venezuela Project, or PV; Democratic Action, or AD; the Social Christian party, or COPEI; Homeland for All, or PPT; and Movement to Socialism, or MAS.

LOCAL GOVERNMENT

Individual states in Venezuela elect their own legislatures, but have limited powers. They operate on funds allocated by the national government and abide by laws and decisions made by the National Assembly on education, health, and agricultural issues. The states are divided into districts and municipalities run by city councils. State governors and council members are elected by their constituents.

THE VENEZUELAN CONSTITUTION

The first Venezuelan constitution was adopted on December 21, 1811, almost six months after independence from Spain. The original document was influenced by, but not based on, the U.S. and French constitutions.

Since 1811 the constitution has been rewritten 25 times, usually in response to political upheaval. The 22nd constitution, adopted in 1945, gave women the right to vote, and the 23rd version, adopted in 1947, separated church from state and increased the authority of the federal government. The 24th constitution, adopted in 1953, changed the country's official name to the Republic of Venezuela. The 25th constitution, adopted in 1999, renamed the country the Bolivarian Republic of Venezuela.

Like the U.S. constitution, the Venezuelan constitution advocates personal liberties and human equality. The introduction states that all Venezuelans have the right to social and legal equality, "without discrimination due to race, sex, creed, or social conditions." One of the constitution's aims is to support democracy as the sole means of ensuring the rights and dignity of citizens. The constitution also refers to Simón Bolívar as the Liberator of Venezuela.

Two articles of the constitution proclaim the right to freedom of religion and expression, and another allows for freedom of peaceful assembly. The constitution requires that the state (the nation of Venezuela) provide an education for all citizens as well as oversee the maintenance of public health. The government promises to try to improve the living conditions of the rural population and to protect the Indian communities and help them integrate into the life of the nation.

In return the constitution declares that the state expects all Venezuelans to "honor and defend their country and to safeguard and protect the interests of the Nation." Military service is compulsory, as is education, and "labor is a duty of every person fit to perform it."

The 1999 constitution ratified the replacement of the senate by a unicameral National Assembly, created the post of vice president, and combined the military forces under one commander—the commander-in-chief, who is the Venezuelan president.

Venezuelan soldiers on parade in Caracas.

THE GOVERNMENT'S GOALS

According to the 1999 constitution the Bolivarian Republic of Venezuela was founded to "establish a society that is democratic, participatory and protagonistic, multi-ethnic and multi-cultural, in a State of justice, federal and decentralized, that consolidates the values of liberty, independence, peace, solidarity, common good, territorial integrity, co-existence and the rule of the law."

SOCIAL MISSIONS

In 2003 President Chávez called for the creation of social programs to tackle problems in areas such as education, health, housing, quality and cost of food, and job training. These programs came to be known as *misiones*—"missions." They are targeted at Venezuela's poorest areas and aim to encourage participation from community members. Some of the social missions include the following:

- **HEALTH** *Mision Barrio Adentro* (Mission Inside the Neighborhood) guarantees access to health services for all citizens. This involves the construction and renovation of various medical centers, clinics, and public hospitals.

HUGO CHÁVEZ

Hugo Rafael Chávez Frias was born in modest origins on July 28, 1954. Both of his parents were schoolteachers and their hometown was Sabaneta, a small farming village in the state of Barinas.

Chávez made his first step forward through sports. He won a baseball scholarship to the Venezuelan Academy of Military Sciences, where he earned a degree in military science and engineering. From there Chávez joined the army and became head of an elite paratrooper unit. It was during this time that he saw the difference between the troops and their corrupt officers. He found more solidarity with the Colombian forces across the border than with Venezuelan military leaders.

Inspired by Simón Bolívar, Chávez created a secret army group called the Bolivarian Revolutionary Movement. The Bolivarian label highlights the similarities between the two Venezuelan leaders, the high ideals, the struggle for all Latin people against "imperialism" and a powerful drive to lead using the force of their rhetoric to energize and draw together the support of the people. It also serves to pass the glory and dignity of the Liberator to the Chávez's rule.

In 1992 Chávez led a coup attempt against the government of Carlos Andres Pérez. Hundreds died and Chávez was jailed for two years, but this was the beginning of his popular image as a hero of the Venezuelan people, fighting a corrupt and unpopular government, proclaiming, "I am convinced that the path to a new, better and possible world is not capitalism, the path is socialism."

Next Chávez sought power through political means. He formed the Polo Patriotico *(Patriotic Pole), a coalition of 14 small political parties from across the political spectrum. Millions of poor Venezuelans supported Chávez (calling him* El Comandanté *—"The Commander") in the hope that he could take political power out of the hands of the upper classes.*

Chávez became the youngest elected president in Venezuelan history on December 6, 1998. He set about the first phase of his Bolivarian revolution by dismantling and reforming the entire government structure of Venezuela. Ever since then he has moved to increase his political power through many laws.

Chávez not only won the elections in 2000, but his supporters also won the majority of seats in the new unicameral National Assembly. This allowed him the freedom to pass laws to reform the country from a capitalist economy to a socialist one. In 2001 he passed a set of 49 economic laws, causing anger and fear among wealthy landowners and middle-class businesspeople. Chávez refuted these claims in an interview: "Some sectors, from ignorance or prejudice, keep saying that in Venezuela there is a process of concentration of power under way. The truth is we are doing away with an authoritarian model that was disguised as a democracy. Representative democracy failed completely in the past. Party leaders, who said they represented the people, betrayed them. I want you to understand the battle we are waging. It's a revolution."

Chávez uses the media in every possible way to spread his message and to suppress the voices of those who oppose him. He deliberately causes controversy through his strong language, support of those he sees as "anti-imperialists," and attacks on "imperialists." Chávez was famously told to "shut up" by King Juan Carlos of Spain in a visit in 2007. He has called Mexico "the puppy dog of the USA." He has also denounced Colombia for "spitting in the face of Venezuela" during a hostage crisis in Venezuela. He called U.S. President George W. Bush "the Devil" as well as "a drunk, an alcoholic, a liar," and "a donkey." He presented Zimbabwean President Robert Mugabe with a replica of Simón Bolívar's sword, calling him "a freedom fighter."

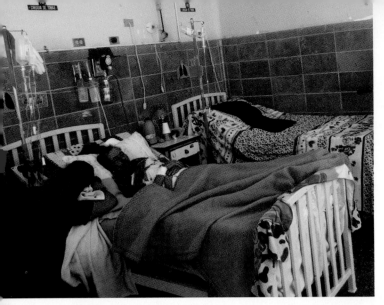

The policies of the Venezuelan government have benefitted many low-income families, such as this patient in a public hospital.

- **EDUCATION** Three missions supply funds to ensure that places in education are funded. Mission Robinson is aimed at the elimination of illiteracy and the completion of a primary education. Mission Ribas allows Venezuelans to complete their high school education by providing remedial classes to students who have dropped out. Mission Sucre provides free degree-level programs.

- **HOUSING** *Mision Habitat* (Mission Habitat) offers credits and aid for the purchase of homes. The mission also aids in the creation of integrated communities, where residents have access to all necessary services, from education to health.

- **FOOD SECURITY** *Mision MERCAL* (Mission MERCAL) gives access to basic food products at low prices, while ensuring that food producers are fairly paid.

- **WOMEN** *Mision Madres del Barrio* (Mission Mothers of the Neighborhood) supports housewives with loans that help them become economically self-sufficient.

- **INDIGENOUS RIGHTS** *Mision Guaicaipuro* (Mission Guaicaipuro) gives communal land titles and human rights to Venezuela's numerous indigenous communities.

In 2011 Chávez continued to implement a number of social reforms, including the mission "My Well-Equipped Home." This mission provides loans through the public banks for basic electrical goods such as washing machines and ovens at about half the normal store price. The Venezuelan government made this possible via an agreement with the Chinese company Haier.

In January 2011 Chávez threatened to take over the Venezuelan subsidiary of the Spanish bank BBVA, unless it dealt with clients struggling to pay their mortgages. In May 2009 Chávez nationalized Banco de Venezuela

(Bank of Venezuela), buying it from Spain's banking giant Grupo Santander (Santander Group) for just over $1 billion. This added to several small banks that have been nationalized. Chávez has also nationalized companies in the oil, cement, food, telecommunications, steel, and power industries.

Also in January 2011 Chávez urged militia forces to occupy unused land in wealthy districts in Caracas to provide low-cost housing for low-income families.

Hugo Chávez entertained many observers in 2011 by offering to mediate between the Libyan leader Muammar Gaddafi and the United States, joking that capitalism may have ended life on Mars and speaking out against cosmetic plastic surgery, which is very popular with many Venezuelan women.

Venezuelans exercising their right to vote during the 2010 elections.

INTERNET LINKS

http://venezuela-us.org/politica/

This website from the Venezuelan Embassy in Washington, D.C., provides a clear description of the organization of the Venezuelan government system.

www.state.gov/r/pa/ei/bgn/35766.htm#gov

This website from the U.S. Department of State provides detailed information on the Venezuelan government under Chávez.

http://countrystudies.us/venezuela/36.htm

This website provides detailed information on the Venezuelan governmental system.

ECONOMY

Containers at a port in Puerto Cabello.

4

I N THE LATE 1970S, DURING PRESIDENT
Carlos Andrés Pérez's first term,
Venezuela was at the height of economic
prosperity. Oil revenues were pouring in;
new petrochemical, steel, and hydroelectric
plants were being built; ships from other
countries were lining up at Venezuelan
ports to unload luxury items imported for
caraqueños; and the wealthiest Venezuelans
were traveling abroad on shopping sprees
or leaving to study at foreign universities.

The Venezuelan
economy has
stark divides,
much as the rest
of the nation
does. Growth
in the economy
contrasts
with currency
devaluations and
high inflation.

Fishermen emptying a boat full of freshly caught sardines in Santa Fe.

By the early 1980s the economic scene had completely changed. A worldwide oil glut had reduced Venezuela's oil revenues, crippling the nation's ability to settle its foreign debt; local prices rose dramatically, while salaries were frozen or jobs lost; even food staples such as salt, rice, and sugar became difficult to obtain.

The Venezuelan economy has been dominated by petroleum since the discovery of oil in 1914. Oil revenues formerly made up more than two-thirds of the government's income and more than 90 percent of the country's exports. Such a heavy reliance on petroleum exports meant that when oil revenues fell, the entire economy collapsed. In 2011 petroleum made up 92 percent of export earnings and contributed around 30 percent of gross domestic product (GDP) and 55 percent of the federal budget revenues.

VENEZUELAN ECONOMY

The Venezuelan economy polarizes opinion as much as President Chávez does. There are signs of gloom or reasons to be cheerful, depending on what side of the political divide you sit.

An iron ore mine in Cerro Bolivar, Venezuela.

According to the Venezuelan government, "Venezuela is a country with an extraordinary potential for economic development. It possesses vast natural resources and a population primarily in the productive age. Per capita, Venezuela is one of the richest countries of Latin America today." The economy has been expanding since the strikes that began in 2002. Record government spending helped the economy grow with a 10 percent increase in GDP in 2006, 8 percent in 2007, and 5 percent in 2008, although oil price falls stopped growth in 2009 and 2010. Consumer spending has also increased, but inflation has been high at 32 percent in 2008 and 30 percent in 2010. Chávez closed the unofficial foreign exchange market in 2010 to slow inflation, replacing it with the Transaction System for Foreign Currency Denominated Securities (SITME). In late 2010 Chávez fixed the exchange rate at 4.3 Bolivars per U.S. dollar, but was forced to devalue it again in January 2011.

CURRENCY

The Venezuelan currency is the Bolivar. On January 1, 2008, the Central Bank of Venezuela (BCV) introduced a new Venezuelan currency, the "Strong Bolivar" (*Bolivar Fuerte*), as part of a monetary reconversion. A "Strong Bolivar" equals what used to be 1,000 Bolivares.

FACTS AND FIGURES

Earnings from petrochemicals, oil refining, manufacturing, construction, and trade make up 41.9 percent of Venezuela's GDP. Agricultural products, which make up 4 percent of the GDP, include corn, sorghum, sugarcane, rice, bananas, vegetables, coffee, beef, pork, milk, eggs, and fish. Exports include petroleum, bauxite, aluminum, steel, chemicals, and agricultural and manufactured products. Imports include machinery and equipment, transportation equipment, raw materials, and construction materials. In 2010 Venezuela exported $64.87 billion worth of goods and imported $31.37 billion worth of goods. The country trades mainly with the United States, Puerto Rico, Colombia, China, Mexico, and Brazil. Other trade partners include Japan, France, Germany, the Netherlands, Italy, and Canada.

Oil wells across
Lake Maracaibo.

PETROLEUM AND MINING

Before the discovery of petroleum in Lake Maracaibo, Venezuela was a relatively poor country of farmers, and many consumer goods had to be imported. Once oil was discovered, however, rapid changes took place, bringing immense wealth to the country, though not to most of the people. Foreign companies were invited to exploit Venezuelan oil reserves and to process extracted oil, and the dictators who were in power in Venezuela at the time hoarded the wealth and made handsome profits for themselves.

When Rómulo Betancourt took control of the government in 1959, he used the accumulated profits from the oil industry to fund desperately needed social programs. He directed foreign oil companies to train Venezuelans and to pay a higher percentage of their profits to the Venezuelan government. Before the 1960s most of Venezuela's oil was refined outside the country. Venezuela now has its own refineries, and gas is saved for fuel and other uses.

About 75 percent of the nation's oil comes from the Lake Maracaibo region. Other reserves are in the northern llanos, in the Apure—Barinas river basin in the west, and in the eastern region. These deposits will not last forever, of course, and the government is building its first oil platform offshore in the Gulf of Paria.

The most important natural resource in Venezuela after petroleum is iron ore, much of which is used in the local steel industry, as are nickel, zinc, and coal. Bauxite, discovered in the 1970s, is used in the aluminum industry.

MANUFACTURING AND POWER GENERATION

Venezuela's early attempts at industrial diversification included the manufacture of aluminum products in Ciudad Guayana. Factories in Caracas produce glass, chemicals, leather goods, pharmaceuticals, and processed food. Venezuela also manufactures steel, textiles, clothing, tobacco, paper, and cars, among other products. In 2009 manufacturing contributed 15.4 percent of the country's GDP, and manufacturing output decreased by 8 percent.

Venezuela has huge electric power dams on the Caroní River, and Venezuelans used to enjoy one of the best electrical energy services in Latin America, but the threat of droughts such as those that occurred in 2010 means that power failures sufficient to cause a national emergency are possible.

The Guri Dam at the Caroní River.

AGRICULTURE

Venezuela neglected its agricultural potential during the oil boom in the 1970s. Eggs came from Florida, meat from Argentina, and vegetables from Chile. Although in the 1930s the agricultural sector contributed 70 percent of the GDP, it accounted for only 4 percent of the GDP in 2010, when Venezuela still imported two-thirds of its food. A quarter of Venezuela's food is imported from the United States, and in 2009, $967 million worth of agricultural products were imported.

With the fall in oil prices and the ensuing economic crisis came plans to exploit Venezuela's agricultural potential. Unfortunately, by 2009, only about 10 percent of the population was still engaged in agriculture. Many people had already moved to urban areas in pursuit of jobs away from the soil.

The government is now encouraging people to become farmers by providing them with credit, technical assistance, and machinery, but many young people prefer to stay in the cities. There has been a drive toward self-sustainability, with a rapid increase in the production of many foodstuffs. In 2010 the government announced that there had been a 48 percent increase in lands under cultivation since 1998. The year 2010 also saw the government nationalize the largest agricultural supply and fertilizer companies, now called Agropatria and FertiNitro.

A herd of cattle in the llanos region of Venezuela.

THE VENEZUELAN WORKFORCE

The Venezuelan workforce is made up of about 13.3 million people, with an unemployment rate of around 6.6 percent in 2009. About 64 percent of the workforce is in services, 23 percent in manufacturing, and 13 percent in agriculture. About 12 percent of the workforce belongs to unions, which are particularly strong in the petroleum and public sectors.

The minimum monthly wage will be $360 in September 2011, according to the Venezuelan government. Household incomes have increased for the worst-off sectors of society. The figures are as high as a 29 percent increase for 97.6 percent of the population. However, the percentage of people in the higher-income groups went from 4 percent of the population in 2004 to only 2.4 percent by 2007. This figure represents both those who moved abroad and those whose income decreased.

The class structure in Venezuela is quite rigid. The upper class works mostly in business. Before the 20th century members of this elite group made their money in agriculture. They owned large cocoa, sugar, or coffee plantations, using African and mestizo laborers. Many members of the upper class now own family businesses.

The towering skyscapers in Parque Central of Caracas are testimony to the increasing affluence of Venezuelans living in the city.

Workers load coffee beans into burlap sacks in a coffee cooperative warehouse in Lara.

The middle class has grown considerably since the discovery of petroleum and the subsequent creation of new jobs. Members of the middle class, most of whom are city dwellers, typically work in technology, business management, education, the priesthood, and the government. Most advertising is aimed at middle-class Venezuelans, because they are most likely to buy consumer goods and housing.

The lower class is mostly rural and makes up the majority of the country's population. Members of this class are often employed as subsistence farmers, farmworkers, sharecroppers, domestic servants, or in other manual occupations.

In Caracas members of the lower class often work in factories. To earn more money, many work the night shift over and above the minimum 40-hour week. Others work in the construction industry, which is based in Caracas. Many laborers belong to the Confederation of Venezuelan Workers, a trade union with more than 2.5 million members.

DOING BUSINESS IN VENEZUELA

Venezuelan businesspeople are typically quite sophisticated, well educated, and accustomed to dealing with people from other cultures. They work in modern, air-conditioned offices, using up-to-date technology, and they wear well-cut suits to work every day.

Venezuelan businesspeople are generally more aware of organizational hierarchies than their counterparts in the United States are. In the office Venezuelans show respect for their superiors by, for example, holding the door open for them and never interrupting or arguing with them. Senior executives have the privilege of speaking first in a meeting and making the final decision.

Business discussions are often formal. Venezuelans do not take kindly to impatient foreigners who fidget in their seat, dominate the conversation, or try to force everyone into a quick decision. The typical Venezuelan businessperson takes time to assess issues before voicing an idea, so that he or she can back down or change position without attracting too much attention. Many Americans have a different way of doing business. They pay little attention to rank, "get down to business" as soon as everyone is seated at the conference table, and sell their products or ideas with a lot of vigor and enthusiasm.

Venezuelans work hard, but they also believe in making time for the traditional Latin American siesta, or midday rest. The normal business day in Venezuela begins at 8:00 A.M. and ends at 6:00 P.M., Monday through Friday. There is a two-hour lunch break at noon, and many people go home for a large meal and a quick nap. Stores are usually open from 9:00 A.M. to 1:00 P.M. and then from 3:00 P.M. to 7:00 P.M. Banks remain open to public from 8:30 A.M. to 3:30 P.M. Restaurants also usually stay open through the siesta hours. Many Venezuelans leave work early on Friday afternoons.

Colleagues at work in one of the offices in a Venezuela city.

INTERNET LINKS

http://web.worldbank.org/WBSITE/EXTERNAL/COUNTRIES/LACEXT/ VENEZUELAEXTN/0,,contentMDK:20214769~pagePK:141137~piPK:141 127~theSitePK:331767,00.html

This website from the World Bank provides information on the Venezuelan economy and changes in the Chávez era.

www.vheadline.com

This site contains news and views on Venezuela.

www.economist.com/countries/Venezuela/

This site shows recent articles on Venezuela from *The Economist*.

ENVIRONMENT

A walkway passing through a towering bamboo grove in Hato Pinero located in the llanos.

5

VENEZUELA HAS SOME 116 MILLION acres (47 million ha) of forested and wooded land, 70 percent of which consists of the Amazon Basin in the south of the country. This equates to 54.1 percent of all land.

Each year human activity clears 710,427 acres (287,500 ha) of the country's forests—mangrove and inland swamps, montane and lowland rain forests, dry forests, and other forests. This represents an annual loss of 0.55 percent of the country's total forest cover—one of the highest rates of deforestation in the tropics. Venezuela lost 7.5 percent of its forest and woodlands between 1990 and 2005.

Although there are zones of protected forest scattered throughout Venezuela, the total area protected is only just over 44,776 square miles (116,000 square km). The country's 43 national parks, managed by the National Park Institute (INPARQUES), showcase an impressive variety of natural habitats and species of wildlife. Venezuela has some 2,356 known species of amphibians, birds, mammals, and reptiles. INPARQUES has information offices in all the national parks and restricts access or charges entry fees to some of the parks. Although national park status may not guarantee protection, many parks are valued as tourist destinations. There are thus both environmental and economic motives for the preservation of such parks.

NATURAL RESOURCES

Venezuela is blessed with natural resources such as diamonds, iron ore, and especially petroleum, natural gas, and coal. The country is also one of the world's top bauxite and aluminum producers.

Although much of Venezuela can seem relatively unspoiled, the major cities seem unplanned, chaotic, and heavily polluted. In the center of Caracas, modern buildings next to Plaza Bolívar overshadow this most important of national monuments. The main river running through Caracas, la Guaire, has long been contaminated by streams of industrial pollution that give it an unhealthy multi-hued look. Air quality in the major cities can be very low, mainly due to heavy traffic.

A mangrove swamp at La Restinga National Park in Nueva Esparta is home to many forms of plant and animal life.

It has been estimated that Venezuelan reserves hold 77 billion barrels of oil, 1.2 trillion barrels of bitumen in the Orinoco belt, and 146.8 trillion cubic feet (4.16 trillion cubic m) of natural gas. The country's refineries produce more than 2.472 million barrels of oil a day (as of 2009). Venezuela is the third-largest producer of coal in South America, after Colombia and Brazil. Most of its coal reserves are found near the border with Colombia.

Hydropower is another major natural resource in Venezuela, generating about 73 percent of the country's electricity supply, which was 113.3 billion kilowatt hours in 2007. The rest of the domestic electricity supply is derived from oil and natural gas.

ENVIRONMENTAL LAW

Venezuela's environment ministry is responsible for, among other tasks, managing national parks and conserving wildlife in the country and monitoring and regulating the exploitation of the country's natural resources.

The ministry can punish those whose activities degrade the environment. It seizes equipment belonging to offenders and imposes penalties ranging from imprisonment to fines to community service. The ministry can also authorize activities that yield definite economic and social benefits, provided that they do not harm the environment irreparably. In such cases guarantees and procedures for the repair of environmental damage must be established in advance.

The Environment Act enacted in 1976 promotes both public and private participation in domestic environmental protection and government taking charge of international agreements on biodiversity, climate change, endangered species, hazardous waste, marine life conservation, the nuclear test ban, and ozone layer protection.

PROBLEMS

Venezuela's environmental problems include pollution and deforestation. Nationally important Lake Maracaibo and Lake Valencia have suffered from sewage and other forms of pollution. The deforestation rate is the highest in South America. Pollution from consumption and energy production is high because production is the engine of the economy and consumption is heavily subsidized by the government. Carbon emissions are higher in Venezuela than in its South American neighbors, largely due to its active hydrocarbon industries and heavy energy subsidization. Oil exploration, sewage dumping, and fertilizer runoff cause severe pollution in the country's rivers and lakes.

The use of renewable energy resources, apart from hydropower, is low in Venezuela. The few domestic renewable energy projects that have been successful have used solar energy to supply electricity to remote areas where companies are exploring for new oil reserves. Mining for coal, gold, and minerals is largely unregulated and many operations pose an environmental threat in the states of Zulia, Bolivar, and Amazonas, mainly through toxic chemicals leaking into the river system.

THREATS TO INDIGENOUS LANDS

In 1993 representatives of the 19 Amazonian native groups of Venezuela held the first Congress of Indigenous Peoples of the Amazon. This resulted in the formation of the Organizacion Regional de Pueblos Indigenas de Amazonas (ORPIA), a democratic organization committed to defending and promoting the interests of indigenous peoples. The second Congress was held in October 2008.

Amazonas State is home to 40,000 indigenous people from the Guajibo, Makiritare, Piaroa, Guaiaca, and Yanomami groups. National parks in this state occupy 23,160 square miles (60,000 square km), and only one of these parks is open to the public. Of the 8,000 plant species found in Amazonas, 7,000 are endemic.

Henri Pittier National Park *in the state of Aragua is Venezuela's oldest national park, founded in 1937. It has an area of 416 square miles (1,078 square km).*

Cueva del Guácharo *in Monagas and Sucre has the famous cave of oilbirds and pre-montane and humid forests filled with many animals, notably pumas and yellow-knobbed curassows.*

Turuépano *in Sucre was created to protect the manatee. The last of Venezuela's "mermaids" live in the Gulf of Paria between the island of Turuépano and the mainland.*

Mochima *in Anzoátegui and Sucre is made up of more than 363 square miles (940 square km) of mountainous coast and islands. The Pampero Ecological Foundation aims to protect the park through measuring its resources and levels of use, making recommendations for sustainable levels of exploitation. Many species of tropical fish thrive in the park's waters.*

Médanos de Coro *in Falcón is a compact desert, complete with wind-sculpted dunes.*

Morrocoy *also in Falcón is more than 124 square miles (320 square km) of coral reefs and mangrove swamps. Its beauty and resident flamingos make it very popular with tourists.*

Archipiélago de Los Roques *in Dependencias Federales consists of islands, islets, keys, lagoons, and beaches with rich marine fauna. The Scientific Foundation of Los Roques protects the endangered green turtle on the island of Dos Mosquises Sur (right).*

Laguna de la Restinga, *41 square miles (107 square km) dominated by mangrove swamps, boasts flamingos, pelicans, and scarlet ibis.*

Sierra Nevada *in Mérida and Barinas covers rain forests, high plains, and snowcapped peaks, such as Pico Bolívar. There is a breeding center for the Andean condor here.*

Sierra la Culata *has a valley running north of Mérida into the Andes. In this rocky terrain live jaguars, tapirs, and spectacled bears.*

Parima-Tapirapecó *is the fifth-largest national park in the world at nearly 15,440 square miles (38,290 square km). Most of the Yanomami of Venezuela live here. The Sierra Parima mountains and the headwaters of the Orinoco are features of the park.*

Serranía de la Neblina *contains the world's largest tepui, through which runs the Cañon Grande de Río Baría, one of the deepest canyons in the world.*

El Ávila *in Distrito Federal, Miranda, and Vargas overlooks Caracas and is a popular hiking destination. Many animals, including armadillos and sloths, live here.*

Yurubí *in Yaracuy has cloud forests in the Sierra de Aroa, which conceal orchids, boa constrictors, and red brocket deer, among many other species.*

Sierra de Perijá *in Zulia consists of cloud forests and high plains. This park is inhabited by the capuchin monkey and king vulture.*

Ciénagas del Catatumbo *in Zulia is home to the jabiru stork, blue heron, great egret, and many other birds that live on the delta of the Catatumbo River along Lake Maracaibo.*

Mariusa *in Delta Amacuro is located in the middle of the Orinoco delta. The Warau people inhabit this park's dense jungle.*

Pemon Indians from the southern jungles of Venezuela protest in front of the Brazilian embassy against the placing of the electrical line over their lands, destroying the delicate ecological sytems.

A government decree in Venezuela guarantees the rights of indigenous peoples to their ancestral lands, and in 2007, 11 communal land titles were given to Pume, Yaruru, Karina, and Warao people in the Apure, Anzoategui, and Bolivar states, along with a series of programs to improve community living. This took place under the banner of the Guicapuro Mission. Unfortunately indigenous land rights often tend to be ignored when logging and mining licenses are issued.

One significant development that threatens the welfare of indigenous Indians in Venezuela is the government's decision to exploit mineral and biological resources in the Imataca Forest Reserve, located in Bolivar and Delta Amacuro states. The 13,896-square-mile (36,000-square-km) reserve is home to more than 10,000 Akawaio, Arawako, Karina, and Pemon Indians as well as many species of wildlife, some of them endemic. In 1997 the government signed Decree 1850, which opened up 40 percent of the reserve to industrial mining and logging operations. Chávez ratified Decree 3110 in 2004, called the "Plan of Ordinance and Regulations of Use for the Imataca Forest." It extended the previous decree's exploitation of the reserve. Twelve percent of the surface of the Imataca Forest Reserve is now designated for mixed logging and mining use. Another 60 percent is available for wood logging. This makes a total area of about 6.7 million acres (2.7 million ha).

The indigenous inhabitants, claiming ancestral rights to the land and objecting to pollution and land degradation caused by mining and forestry, have clashed with small- and medium-scale miners and developers who are operating in the area. In 1998 Pemon Indians set up roadblocks in protest to the planned electrical line through the Guayana region, but their bows and arrows were no match for the rubber bullets and tear gas the National Guard used to break up the demonstration. In the next two years the Pemon Indians knocked down 12 pylons, to no avail.

Wood from the reserve makes up 11 percent of Venezuela's total timber production. Currently there are 12 timber concessionaires operating in the reserve, in an area equivalent to 2.9 million acres (1.2 million ha). Significant deposits of gold and diamonds have been identified in the reserve's boundaries. There are at least 300 mining concessions and contracts in the Imataca Forest Reserve, most of which were granted by the government.

In Amazonas State, mining has hurt Yanomami Indians in the Upper Orinoco—Casiquiare Biosphere Reserve, the largest area of protected rain forest in the world. The area is already being illegally exploited by both Venezuelan and Brazilian gold miners. Much of Venezuela's gold is near the surface, making it easy and economical to extract. To get at the gold, miners conveniently clear the topsoil and vegetation by spraying jets of water from powerful pumps that draw water from nearby rivers. Gas and oil exploration in the Orinoco Delta and the Gulf of Paria also disturb the environment, with the potential for greater harm from permanent installations.

Mining has caused deforestation and mercury poisoning in the lands of Kapon and Pemon Indians in Bolívar State. In 1996 several species of fish had to be banned from human consumption due to high levels of mercury detected in the Guri Dam.

INTERNET LINKS

http://rainforests.mongabay.com/20venezuela.htm

This website provides detailed information on Venezuela's rain forests.

http://venezuela-us.org/energy-environment-10/

This site from the Embassy of the Bolivarian Republic of Venezuela provides details about the Venezuelan government's environmental policies.

http://amazonwatch.org/

This site provides information on environmental issues in the Amazon region.

VENEZUELANS

A multigenerational mestizo family unit in Venezuela.

6

VENEZUELANS ARE UNITED IN language, religion, and loyalty to their country. From the blue-eyed, blond-haired descendants of German immigrants to the dark-eyed, dark-haired descendants of indigenous Indians, all are *Venezolanos* (beh-neh-zoh-LAH-nohs). From Latin last names such as Martinez and Pérez to European last names such as Jordan and Vollmar, all belong to *Venezolanos*.

Venezuelan children in the Lara State live simpler lives than their city neighbors.

Venezuelan pride in the national image is embodied in the steady stream of Miss Worlds and Miss Universes the country has produced. To the contestants the pageants are a stepping-stone to international fame and career success, but not always only as models.

Venezuelans have racially intermarried since colonial times. A 69 percent majority are mestizos, people of mixed ethnicity. Mestizos live throughout the country, in both urban and rural areas. People of European descent, mostly Spanish and German, make up 20 percent of the population. They live mainly in the cities. People of African origin make up 9 percent of the population, and indigenous Indians make up the remaining 2 percent of the population. Most African Venezuelans live in the northern coastal regions, while Indians live in the south or on the Colombian border.

About 2 percent of the Venezuelan population is made up of legal immigrants. It is estimated that there are more than 2 million illegal immigrants in the country. Most are Colombians who work in the construction industry in Caracas or in the petroleum industry in Maracaibo.

POPULATION DISTRIBUTION

In 2011 there were 27.6 million people living in Venezuela. The country experienced a population boom in the 1920s, after the discovery of petroleum in Maracaibo, and again in the 1950s. After World War II, the availability of jobs in Venezuela attracted more than 500,000 immigrants from Italy, Spain, Portugal, France, Poland, and Germany.

Oil revenues have given the Venezuelan people better health-care services. This has helped lower the country's death rate while maintaining a high birthrate. Whereas in the 1930s, 18 in 1,000 Venezuelans died each year, by 2011 the annual death rate had dropped to 5.7 in 1,000.

Venezuela's birthrate at the start of the 21st century was 21 in 1,000, falling to 20 in 1,000 in 2011, as compared with 17.2 in 1,000 for Chile and about 19 in 1,000 for Argentina and Brazil. Life expectancy is about 73 years; most Venezuelans die of "modern" diseases such as heart disease, rather than contagious diseases that still cause many deaths in less developed countries.

The Venezuelan population grew annually by 3.6 percent in the 1960s; by 2011 the growth rate had fallen to 1.5 percent. Despite family planning encouraged by the government, the population growth rate remains high.

Between 1995 and 2000 Venezuela's urban population grew by more than 2 percent, whereas the rural population declined. The prediction for 2010 to

2015 is for a slower growth rate of 1.7 percent. The cities and towns, each with more than 1,000 people, support 93 percent of the national population. Only 7 percent of Venezuelans live in the rural areas.

CLASS STRUCTURE

For centuries a deep-rooted class structure divided Venezuelan society into just two classes of people: the wealthy Europeans and the rest. Before the discovery of oil in the 1920s, about 70 percent of Venezuelans were illiterate rural peasants. By the 1980s demographic trends had reversed, with more than 80 percent of the population in the literate urban category. The move away from traditional society sped up in the 1940s, with a burgeoning middle class.

A group of friends living in Mérida. Nearly 90 percent of Venezuelans live in cities and towns.

Class distinctions persist in modern Venezuela, and there is a wide gap between the rich and the poor. Wealth, family background, and cultural accomplishments set the minority upper class apart. Their ethnic heritage is European, and many of them are well educated and well traveled. The women are very elegant; few of them pursue careers, and most have household servants.

The middle class is made up of educated people of mixed ethnic backgrounds. Much of their social life revolves around their occupations. Manual laborers and farmers make up the lower class. They often live in small villages, forming close-knit communities. Social life revolves around planting, harvesting, and religious ceremonies.

GERMANY IN VENEZUELA

In the 1830s, after wars stripped the countryside of farmers and slaves, the Venezuelan government encouraged people from Europe to migrate to

A church in Colonia Tovar, a town in a fertile valley.

Venezuela. Two mapmakers, Agustín Codazzi from Italy and Alexander Benitz from Germany, came up with an idea to send a group of German peasants to an area near Caracas, where they could settle down and hopefully prosper. The desired land belonged to a wealthy aristocrat named Manuel Felipe de Tovar. Tovar donated the piece of land to the establishment of the new colony, Colonia Tovar.

A school, church, and pharmacy were built, and a printing press brought in to publish news in Spanish and German. Benitz recruited people from the Schwarzwald, or Black Forest, in Germany. Envisioning a completely self-sufficient colony, Benitz selected artisans, doctors, teachers, and farmers to form the migrant community. A group of 374 men, women, and children set out for Venezuela in 1843. Unfortunately 70 of them died of smallpox on board the ship.

The remaining immigrants landed on an open beach. There were no roads leading up the mountains to their destination, so they had to climb on foot. More died along the way, but the survivors found a glorious place with a perfect climate waiting for them. They soon settled down and waited for more of their countrymen to join them. Unfortunately none came, and the new colonists were forgotten by the Venezuelan government. They remained isolated for more than 80 years and retained the German language and customs they had brought with them. Only in 1963 was a proper road built from Caracas, making Colonia Tovar more accessible.

Colonia Tovar is now a popular tourist destination as well as an agricultural center. Venezuelans and foreigners visit the town to see Bavarian-style architecture, watch authentic German dances, and eat German sausage, sauerkraut, Black Forest cake, and locally cultivated strawberries, apples, and peaches.

THE INDIANS OF VENEZUELA

From around a million people before the Spanish conquest, the indigenous population has dwindled to about 523,743, making up just 1.9 percent of the national population. Many of Venezuela's indigenous Indians live in the most inaccessible areas, such as the Orinoco delta, the rain forests that spread south into Brazil and west into Colombia, and the desert-like Guajira Peninsula just north of Maracaibo.

Guajiro Indians make up the largest indigenous group in Venezuela. They speak their own language, wear distinctive colorful clothes, and follow ancient customs and rituals. Some, however, have left their desert homes to pursue jobs in Maracaibo. These have assimilated into urban society, working in the oil and construction industries, or selling fruits and vegetables at outdoor markets.

Guajiro Indian women at a street market in the state of Zulia.

A young girl from the Yanomami Indian tribe with her decorative painted face, flower-adorned ears, and thin bamboo piercings.

Those who stay in their homeland lead a semi-nomadic lifestyle; they live in temporary homes, which they leave when food and water run out. Many Guajiros have intermarried, but they retain their culture and identity, and many children of mixed marriages think of themselves as Guajiro rather than mestizo. Guajiros educated in the city often return to the peninsula to resume their former way of life.

At least 12 different Indian groups live in the Amazonas Federal Territory near the Brazilian border. Each has its own language and culture.

The Makiri-tare or Yekuana people live on rivers and use 54-foot-long (16.5-m-long) dugout canoes made from tree trunks as transportation vehicles. The Piaroa build 36-foot-high (11-m-high) conical houses thatched with palm fronds. The warlike Yanomami are one of the most isolated groups in Venezuela and Brazil. Many of them have never seen a human being with fair skin. Warau Indians live in the Orinoco River delta. They are skilled fishermen and navigators, and build their homes on stilts.

DRESS HABITS

In Caracas and other large cities, upper- and upper-middle-class people dress conservatively. The men wear suits, white shirts, and ties; the women wear dresses, skirts and blouses, or suits. Businesswomen wear makeup and dress elegantly, with jewelry and high heels, but they never wear revealing clothing.

At night people dress formally for dining out or going to the theater. Men wear jackets and ties while women wear cocktail dresses, often with designer labels. Jeans and casual clothing are worn on the streets. Shorts are frowned upon, except at the beach or on the tennis court. Few people wear hats.

Working-class city dwellers usually wear inexpensive cotton clothes. The men are often seen in light-colored shirts open at the neck, paired with khaki pants, while the women wear print dresses, skirts, and blouses.

Children dress nicely for Mass on Sundays, as parents take pride in how their children look. Little girls often wear bright-colored ruffled dresses to

Mass. Many of them have their ears pierced, and they wear gold jewelry. All children wear uniforms to school. In the poorest areas some toddlers may walk around without any clothing.

In rural areas men often wear straw hats in hot weather and felt ones in cooler weather. Lower-class men often wear pants cut off at the knees and sandals. Some go barefoot. Upper-class men wear boots or shoes, but rarely dress in formal jackets and ties.

During the holidays in the lowlands, men wear traditional *liqui-liqui* (lih-kih-LIH-kih), white cotton shirts and pants fastened with leather or gold buttons or a sash. Women wear colorful full skirts called *joroperas* (hoh-roh-PAY-rahs) with elaborately embroidered off-the-shoulder blouses.

While Guajiro men often dress in plain fashion, wearing only a shirt, loincloth, and straw hat, Guajiro women usually wear flowing, floor-length mantas sewn in stunning colors. The Guajiros are also expert weavers of bright-colored saddle-bags and belts.

Young girls wearing pretty, dressy outfits for Sunday Mass sit together at a beach in Macuto.

INTERNET LINKS

www.buzzle.com/articles/venezuela-facts.htm/

This site contains some interesting and fun facts about Venezuela.

www.cia.gov/library/publications/the-world-factbook/geos/ve.html

This website provides a collection of up-to-date facts from the Central Intelligence Agency's World Factbook on Venezuela.

http://venezuela-us.org/comunidades-indigenas-venezolanas

This site from the Venezuela U.S. embassy includes information on the main Venezuelan indigenous communities.

LIFESTYLE

These brightly painted houses in the historic center of Bolívar city are equipped with modern telephone lines, street lighting, and paved roads for the everyday commute.

7

DESPITE EXTREME CONTRASTS IN lifestyles across regions, there is a distinct Venezuelan personality and culture. The Venezuelan identity is shaped by the unique ways in which Venezuelans live, spend their days, and communicate.

GETTING BY OR LIVING IT UP?

Lifestyle variations in Venezuela are nowhere near as evident as in the living conditions in different regions. Venezuelans live in extremely different worlds: those who live in cities versus those who live in villages; those who live in houses or apartments versus those who live in shacks; those who are rich versus those who are poor.

A view of the ranchos in the ghetto district of Caracas.

Venezuelan families are difficult to characterize because they contain elements of both a patriarchal influence and a matriarchal influence, through the mother and grandmother. Boys are pampered and men have freedoms given to them in a still macho society. Families tend to be close and children can stay at home until their twenties or thirties. Grandparents may also live in the family home. The difficulty of finding available and affordable housing means that families stay together for longer and longer.

Housing variations are particularly apparent in the big cities, especially Caracas, which suffers from an acute housing shortage. Periods of economic growth have drawn people to the capital city in search of jobs. Although many have found employment, few have found affordable housing.

Only the wealthiest *caraqueños* live in single-family homes, which are usually spacious, with a garden, swimming pool, and balcony. The house in Venezuela may not be the family's only property; the elite of Caracas often also have beach homes and apartments in North America.

Most of the middle and upper classes live in high-rise apartment buildings. The typical apartment comes with bedrooms, a kitchen, a bathroom, a living room, and a balcony. Many have servants' quarters, while the nicer buildings also have swimming pools.

Housing costs in Caracas are extremely high, comparable to those in New York, Tokyo, or Rio. Although the government has constructed some public housing in Caracas, demand still far exceeds supply. Hence the poorest *caraqueños* have had to build shanties on the hilly outskirts of the city where they can live rent-free.

Pedestrians stroll along the Sabana Grande shopping district in front of the Bazar Bolívar department store in downtown Caracas.

SPANISH ARCHITECTURE

Many Venezuelan homes have a distinctly Spanish look. Elegant houses built in colonial times have rooms built around a patio garden, a wall surrounding the house to guard the family's privacy, fancy iron gates and hardwood doors, bright-colored flowers in bloom hanging from a roof made from traditional dark-brown Spanish tiles, and walls painted in vibrant colors such as lemon yellow, fuchsia, and emerald green.

In many small towns in Venezuela, buildings and roads are arranged in a pattern that the Spanish colonists brought with them centuries ago. The town plan throughout the Spanish New World had government and religious buildings bordering the central plaza and streets laid out perpendicular to one another to give a sense of balance and harmony.

The central plaza, which served as the marketplace, was flanked by the most important public buildings and the residences of the most influential citizens. The houses of government officials and businessmen stood just off the square. Townspeople in the lowest classes lived the farthest away from the plaza.

THE FAMILY UNIT

In Venezuela the family unit is more important than any of its individual members. Each member acknowledges and appreciates the essential role that every other member plays in the family. The children respect and revere their father as the head of the household and their mother as the manager of domestic affairs. Grandparents often form part of the household and are treated with respect. Even when the children grow up, marry, and move away, they maintain close contact with their family and return home whenever they are needed.

In many Latin American cultures, the family circle is extended through the appointment of godparents: a *comadre* (kom-MAH-dray), or "co-mother," and a *compadre* (kom-PAH-dray), or "co-father." The godparents are supposed to guide their godchildren's religious and moral education. Parents usually ask only close friends whom they trust and admire to be their children's

Many Venezuelan customs and attitudes can be traced back to the colonial period.

Ranchos, or shanties, are also found in the rural areas. The walls of rural ranchos are made from poles or bamboo, overlaid with palm fronds or mud. The roof is thatched with palm fronds, and the floor may be made from wooden planks. Kerosene lamps provide artificial light, and water is brought in from a nearby stream or well. Most of these homes have only two rooms: a kitchen and a living room or bedroom.

Oil- or wood-burning stoves are used in the kitchen. Rooms can easily be added as the family grows. Rancho dwellers sleep in hammocks, or chinchorros (chin-CHOR-rohs), which are hung from large hooks in the walls. Chinchorros are comfortable and easy to store. The family may share the sleeping area with their pets and livestock such as chickens and goats.

godparents. Often the godparents act as sponsors for their godchildren, contributing money to the First Communion ceremony, for instance, or helping their godchildren make connections when seeking employment later in life.

THE VENEZUELAN MAN AND THE LLANERO

The typical Venezuelan man has a traditional view of life. He is the chief—and often the sole—wage earner and makes all the family decisions. He prefers his wife not to work, as this would imply that he cannot provide adequately for the family. Venezuelan men are quite conscious of the image they present to society. They would never wish to appear weak or unmasculine or be dominated by their wives.

The typical Venezuelan man regards the cowboy of the llanos, or the *llanero*, as a hero. The *llanero* does not exist only in Venezuelan folklore; he lives in the sparsely populated central region of the country, where the seasons alternate between flood and drought. The *llanero* is famed for his courage and strength. The legendary *llanero* drank nothing but a cup of strong coffee in the morning and spent his day on a half-wild horse, rounding up his herd with a lasso and driving the cattle to be branded. In the wet season, he followed his cattle in a canoe; in the dry season, he drove them across the plains in a cloud of heat and dust.

After an exhausting day, the *llanero* sat by the fire with his companions and talked about the events of the day over a hearty meal. Playing his *cuatro* (KWAH-troh), a four-stringed guitar, the *llanero* danced and sang about the suffering of his Indian ancestors. At the end of the day, he hung up his hammock to sleep and recharge for the next sunrise.

Venezuelan cowboys herding cattle on horseback in llanos. The *llanero* leads a solitary existence. His motto is: "I, on my horse, above me my hat, above my hat, God." He is free and indomitable and lives by muscle and determination to battle nature.

THE VENEZUELAN WOMAN

Venezuelan women—like most Latin American women—tend to be conservative. Many Latin American women do not go out alone or even in groups at night unless accompanied by male companions such as their father or their brothers. Younger Venezuelan women will go to considerable lengths to look glamorous and attractive. The beauty and cosmetic surgery industries are highly advanced and attract clients from other Latin American countries and overseas. Venezuelans take pride in their impressive record in international beauty pageants and this creates a reputation to live up to.

Most Latin American women hope to get married and raise children. Within the home they see themselves as administrators, overseeing the household budget, the housework, the children's religious upbringing, and the family's social activities. Children treat their mothers with unreserved affection; they are often not as openly affectionate with their fathers, the disciplinarians.

Wives and mothers are very concerned with cleanliness in the home and with personal hygiene. They bathe their children two to three times a day and dress them in freshly washed and pressed clothes for dinner.

WOMEN IN THE WORKFORCE

Economic development and urbanization have created employment opportunities for Venezuelan women. The female percentage of the country's workforce has risen from less than 20 percent in 1950 to more than 40 percent in the late 1990s. In 2002, 81 percent of women were employed. Fewer women are leaving the workforce after marriage; more women between ages 35 and 44 are entering or staying in the workforce. The Women's Development Bank (*Banco de la Mujer,* or *Banmujer*) was set up in 2001 to provide loans and educational workshops to women's cooperatives to strengthen women's economic position.

More women have moved from rural areas to the cities and found a broader range of jobs open to them, including domestic and factory work. More women are entering professional and technical fields, building careers as doctors, lawyers, dentists, architects, teachers, laboratory technicians, nurses, and government officials. The 1989 presidential elections saw the country's first woman candidate, Ismenia Villaba. Women hold 18.6 percent of the seats in the National Assembly. A former Miss Universe winner, Irene Sáez, was mayor of the Chacao district of Caracas before she became one of three main candidates for the presidency in 1998. She was governor of the state of Nueva Esparta, which comprises the islands of Margarita, Coche, and Cubagua.

Women of the upper classes often devote themselves to charitable causes, supporting adult literacy programs and cultural institutions such as museums

Elementary school classroom with teacher and students in Caracas, Venezuela.

and ballet companies. It is a matter of pride for them to go to college, even if they have no intention of working after graduation. More than 50 percent of the students enrolled in universities in Venezuela in 1990 were women.

Despite having achieved high levels of professional success and financial independence, many Venezuelan women still choose to promote their femininity and avoid appearing aggressive or competitive.

CHILDREN

Most Venezuelan babies and children are well cared for, whether they are born into upper- or lower-class families. Small children receive a lot of attention from all members of the extended family. Little girls are encouraged to be motherly toward their younger siblings and passive when interacting with boys their age. As children grow, girls are watched more closely than are their brothers, who are given fewer responsibilities and more freedom.

EDUCATION

In the past only upper-class Venezuelans had access to formal education. School was thought to be unnecessary for middle- and lower-class children, who took manual jobs. Rómulo Betancourt's government, which took office in 1959, was the first to place emphasis on education. Educational material was brought in, teacher-training programs were developed, and some 2,287 new schools were built throughout the country in just five years.

Total school enrolment in 1958 was 845,000; by 2007 it was 2.2 million. The literacy rate, which was just over 50 percent in the 1950s, reached 82 percent by the 1970s and 93 percent in 2010.

Today 93 percent of Venezuelan children attend school; 15 percent attend private, church-related primary and secondary schools. Public education from kindergarten through university is free. Some children in the most remote areas have only a one-room schoolhouse and an undertrained teacher to report to, while some have no school to go to at all. About 195,000 children have not been to a primary school, according to a UNESCO report in 2010.

Public school students usually attend classes in shifts. Some go to school from early in the morning until about 1:30 p.m. and others attend from early afternoon until about 6:00 P.M. All schoolchildren wear uniforms.

Venezuelan education starts at the preschool level, and can be roughly divided into nursery school (under age four) and kindergarten (ages four to six). Basic education (grades one through six) lacks a general national governing program outside of the math curriculum. English is taught at a basic level throughout basic education. Upon completing basic education, students are given a Basic Education Certificate.

Middle education (grades seven through nine) explores each one of the sciences as a subject and algebra. English education continues and schools may have a choice in offering either ethics or Catholic religion. Once students complete ninth grade, they enter diversified education, so called because the student must choose between studying humanities and the sciences for the next two years. Some schools may include professional education, and instead award the title of *Técnico en Ciencias* (Technician of the Sciences).

Primary school children in Venezuela study subjects similar to those that their counterparts in the United States study. These include reading, writing, arithmetic, natural science, history, geography, and civics.

After six years of primary school, students attend a four-year program in science and the humanities, with English and ethics or Catholic studies. A second program includes either humanities such as philosophy, literature, or sciences such as physical science, mathematics, and biology. Successful students receive the title of Bachelor of Humanities or Bachelor of Sciences. Secondary school students can attend technical schools for instruction in industry, commerce, nursing, and social welfare. Successful students will be awarded the title of Technician of the Sciences.

Approximately 860,000 Venezuelan students are enrolled in university programs in the country. Most of them study economics, business, engineering, law, and health. Leading public universities include the Central University of Venezuela, founded in 1725; Los Andes University; and Simón Bolívar University. The government also administers extensive adult literacy and job-training programs.

The landscaped courtyard of the Los Andes University in Merida.

SOCIAL GRACES

The big Venezuelan cities have become more internationally oriented since the oil boom and the influx of foreigners. The United States in particular has made a significant impact on Venezuelan society, but not so much that Venezuelans—especially those of the upper classes—have given up their social rituals.

Venezuelan society is essentially hierarchical. Rank is very important. Older people come before younger people; people with titles wield more influence than those without; members of the upper class may be served in a restaurant before middle-class diners who arrived first. When someone holds a title such as doctor or professor, it is important to use it when addressing him or her.

Receiving an invitation to a Venezuelan home is considered something of an honor. The home is a refuge, a place where only the extended family and closest friends are welcome. Guests who fall into neither of these categories are treated formally. In a small party, the guest is introduced by the host or hostess and is expected to greet, shake hands with, and say "good-bye" to each of the other guests individually. At large gatherings, the guests introduce themselves to one another. The casual "hi, everybody" and "take care" that Americans arrive and leave with would be considered undignified at a Venezuelan gathering.

Certain subjects of conversation are taboo at dinner parties, especially for foreigners. It is considered impolite to gossip or spread rumors about well-known personalities, to discuss politics, to tell political jokes, or to talk about the problem of illegal aliens from Colombia. Controversial subjects are not raised, as arguing must be avoided at all costs. Venezuelans do not like being asked personal questions about marriage or family, for instance, until they know the person fairly well.

Venezuelans make social calls to admire a new baby or house or to thank a host or hostess for dinner. However, they do not visit between 1:00 and 4:00 P.M., as the siesta hours are a time to nap, read, or write letters. In the United States neighbors often drop in on a newcomer to welcome him or her to the area. In Venezuela it is just the opposite. Newcomers call on the established members of the community to introduce themselves.

In Venezuela a cup of coffee is the symbol of hospitality. It is offered during a social call, after dinner, or at the start of a business meeting. It is considered rude to decline a cup of coffee, but it is acceptable to drink only one or two sips. There are two rules when the bill arrives after a meal: The person who made the invitation pays for everyone, and the man never lets the woman pay.

TAKING TIME

Venezuelans like to take their time. If they arrive late for an appointment, it may be because they were taking time to be courteous at a previous meeting. Venezuelans have a relaxed attitude toward tardiness. In Caracas, where traffic jams are common, delays are considered a part of life, and *caraqueños* accept them casually, even cheerfully. When entering an office or a shop, it is more important to stop and greet the receptionist or shopkeeper than to rush about accomplishing something. A smile or nod is all that is required.

In business Venezuelans take their time to assess a situation before offering an idea or making a decision. Personal relationships also progress slowly and carefully. Venezuelans are not likely to appreciate an impatient businessperson who demands an immediate answer or an acquaintance who asks intimate questions.

THE LIFE CYCLE

Most significant life events in Venezuela are outwardly similar to those in other countries where the main religion is Roman Catholicism. There are some differences, however, in the way Venezuelans celebrate birthdays, the coming-of-age events, weddings, and funerals, which give meaningful insights into their cultural identity.

Neighbors in Caracas enjoying a chat as they play with their children.

BIRTH The birth of a child is a time of great rejoicing. Relatives and close family friends flock to the home of the newborn to celebrate the arrival. Traditionally older people bring a strong homemade liquor to toast the baby's health.

In general boys are preferred, since they are easier to bring up than girls. For instance there is no need to chaperone a boy when he goes out. Upper-class Venezuelans often choose to have big families with eight or nine children. Poor families sometimes have even more. Most middle-class couples are well informed about family planning and opt for a small family with only two or three children.

In 1992 Venezuela's birthrate was 27 in 1,000; in 2011 it was 20 in 1,000. This is still a high birthrate, even though fewer babies are being born.

BIRTHDAYS Venezuelans throw parties to celebrate their children's birthday. The highlight of children's birthday parties is often the piñata, a bright-colored figure in the shape of a man or animal that is stuffed with toys and candy. Blindfolded, all the children at the party take turns trying to hit the piñata with a stick until it breaks open releasing its contents. There are entire shops in Venezuela selling nothing but piñatas and toys and candy to put in them.

Piñatas on sale in Caracas. No birthday celebration is complete without one.

THE 15TH BIRTHDAY When Venezuelan girls reach the age of 15, many have a *quinceañera* (kin-say-ah-nee-AIR-ah), a special 15th birthday party. This ritual, a Latin form of the debutante or "coming out" party, is common in many South American cultures. It announces to society that the girl is now a woman and is ready to join the social world. In the past the purpose of the *quinceañera* was to bring the girl into contact with eligible men, but this has become an obsolete function in modern South American countries, where boys and girls interact in social situations from an early age. The scale of expenses varies: Poorer families may invite a hundred or so guests, while wealthy families have been known to invite thousands. Most parties are held in a club or hall. For wealthy families the party is usually held at home. The larger celebrations can cost a great deal and can put the family in debt for years.

The party begins at about 9:00 P.M. and can last until dawn, but usually ends at about 2:00 A.M. Dinner and drinks are served, although the birthday girl is usually only allowed a sip of champagne from her father's glass. For dessert, there is usually a large cake. In wealthy families, it is multi-tiered like a wedding cake.

Girls and women often wear fancy ball gowns, and boys and men wear either nice suits or tuxedos. There is often a band, and the birthday girl traditionally dances the first dance, which is likely to be a waltz, with her father. Then she dances with her male peers. It is considered a status symbol to give a fancy *quinceañera*. In the big cities the party will often be covered in the newspapers.

WEDDINGS Wedding parties are often grand affairs. Like *quinceañeras*, weddings are an opportunity to invite many guests and to show society that no expense is spared in celebrating a milestone in the life of a daughter. Among the upper classes it is considered good luck if the bride and groom can sneak away from the wedding celebration within a few hours of its commencement without being noticed.

FUNERALS Funerals are solemn occasions. Often, after the ceremony, family members gather at the home of the departed to comfort the family. The wife of a deceased man usually wears black for a long time, if she is religious. Some widows even wear black for the rest of their lives. Less traditional or younger widows are not likely to wear black at all. Widowers often wear dark clothes for a week or month.

Newlyweds posing outside their church in Venezuela.

INTERNET LINKS

www.everyculture.com/To-Z/Venezuela.html

This site provides useful information, rather than statistics, on Venezuela and Venezuelans.

www.carnaval.com/venezuela/queens/

This site contains all you would want to know about Venezuela's beauty queens.

www.country-studies.com/venezuela/social-structure.html

This website provides information on Venezuelan social structure from Country Studies.

www.kwintessential.co.uk/resources/global-etiquette/venezuela-country-profile.html

This site includes information on good etiquette in Venezuela.

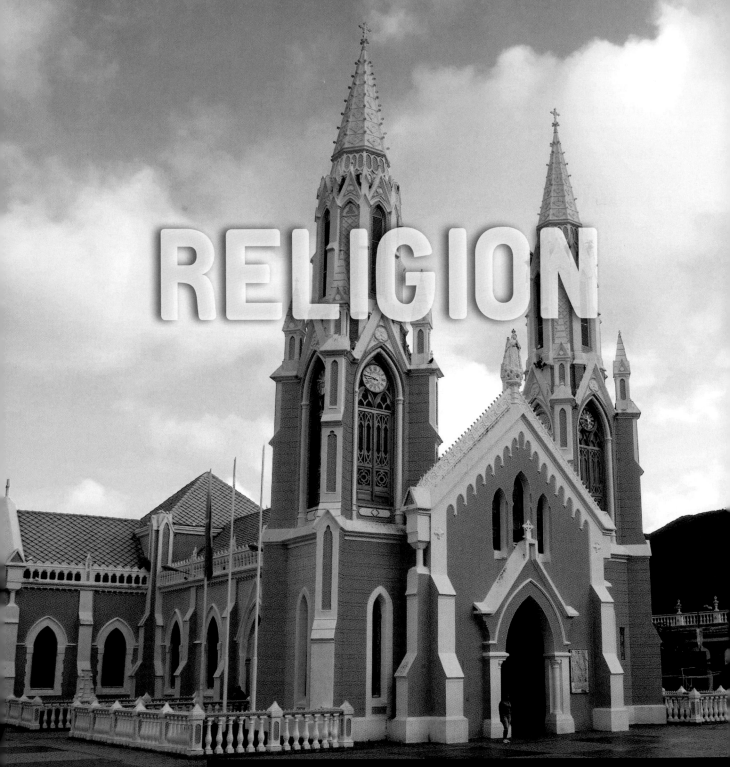

RELIGION

The facade of the Basilica Virgen del Valle church on Margarita Island.

8

T HE OFFICIAL RELIGION of Venezuela is Roman Catholicism, although the constitution guarantees freedom of religion. In 2000, 96 percent of Venezuelans were Catholic, 2 percent Protestant, and the remaining 2 percent followers of other religions.

The Spanish brought Catholicism to Venezuela. In 1513 Dominican and Franciscan priests came to northeastern Venezuela to develop coffee, sugar, and cocoa plantations and to teach indigenous Indians cattle breeding. Capuchin missionaries founded 100 stations in the llanos

The stone chapel by artist Juan Félix Sánchez in Mucuchies is dedicated to Our Lady of Coromoto.

There is a strong missionary aspect to Venezuela's Catholic Church, and an important part of church work is carried out overseas. In Venezuela joining the priesthood is not seen as a good career move so the priests who celebrate Mass and hear confessions often come from other Catholic countries. Mass is given in Spanish and there may be a variety of interesting accents.

The entrance to the unusual Iglesia de San Antonio in Clarines. This old Spanish church is believed to have been constructed in the 1750s.

between 1658 and 1758, while Jesuits were active in the Orinoco River areas. They were quite successful in converting the locals and in building and running religious schools throughout the country.

Although the Catholic Church in Venezuela is not formally linked to the state, it does receive financial support from the government in the form of salaries for some church officials and subsidies for church building maintenance. The Church also consults the government when naming powerful church officials, and church representatives often attend important secular functions, such as the opening of a power plant.

Venezuela has many beautiful Catholic churches; there is at least one in each town. Many are modeled after the Cathedral of Coro on the Caribbean coast and La Asuncíon on Margarita Island, both completed in 1617. Architectural ornamentation is minimal.

CATHOLIC BELIEFS AND TRADITIONS

Roman Catholics believe that the pope is the supreme leader of the Church. According to Catholic tradition, the present-day pope is the latest in a succession of popes starting with Saint Peter, who was appointed by Jesus Christ as the cornerstone of the Church. The pope is believed to be infallible in making decisions on matters of the faith. Roman Catholics receive six of seven sacraments, or signs of grace, to develop spiritually.

BAPTISM   A baby is baptized to be cleansed of "original sin," or sin inherited from the disobedience of Adam and Eve, the father and mother of the human race, according to Christian beliefs. Baptism gives each newborn a fresh start in life and allows the baby to become a member of the Church. This sacrament is performed by a priest, who pours water over the baby's forehead while saying, "I baptize you in the name of the Father and of the Son and of the Holy Spirit."

Baptism marks a milestone in the life of every individual entering the Catholic faith, regardless of social class. Venezuelans who live in remote areas of the country, away from parish centers, travel long distances to have their babies baptized. Poorer parents may have to wait until they can raise enough money for a proper christening party or choose godparents who are willing and able to contribute money. In wealthier families, christening parties can be elaborate affairs.

CONFIRMATION   Most Catholics are confirmed between the ages of 12 and 18 in a ritual ceremony. Confirmation is the sacrament that seals the faith received at baptism. It indicates that the person is now an adult and is responsible for his or her own religious life. Confirmed Catholics have a duty to live out their faith through prayer and acts of charity.

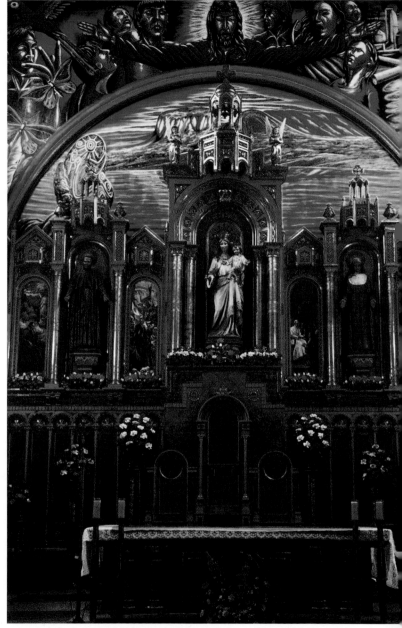

The ornate altar in the Cathedral of Maria Auxiliadora in Plaza Bolívar.

Items of worship at the altar of the religious art museum in Caracas.

HOLY EUCHARIST Also called Holy Communion, this sacrament serves as a channel for spiritual nourishment. Catholics believe that Jesus Christ exists in the bread and wine consecrated on the altar at every Mass. The first part of the Mass consists of readings from the scriptures; the second part focuses on the Holy Eucharist. When Catholics ingest the bread and wine, they believe they receive the body and blood of Christ, the source of life. Before receiving the sacrament, they are expected to meditate and pray and to have fasted for an hour before the Mass. Catholic children make their First Holy Communion at about the age of seven, when they are believed to know the difference between right and wrong.

PENANCE This sacrament entails the confession of sins. A confessor enters a box-like cubicle inside the church and reveals to a priest, who represents God, the sins he or she has committed. The priest then forgives the person in the name of God and assigns the confessor a penance: the recitation of certain prayers or performance of a ritual to atone for the sins confessed.

MATRIMONY Among Catholics marriage is a sacred bond that unites a couple and allows them to have children. Catholic marriages should not be broken by divorce, although divorce does happen in Venezuela, as it does in many countries.

ANOINTING OF THE SICK This sacrament is performed on the very sick and the dying. Also known as last rites, the anointing of the sick brings forgiveness to the dying and prepares them for entry into heaven. The priest applies olive oil—symbolic of light, strength, and life—on the forehead of the recipient and asks for God's forgiveness of all sins committed by the person through sight, touch, taste, smell, and hearing.

HOLY ORDERS This sacrament applies only to priests. It is performed by a bishop, who lays his hands on the candidate for priesthood and gives him the power to minister the other sacraments, such as Holy Eucharist and Holy Matrimony. Only men can become priests in the Catholic Church; they take a vow of celibacy, promising to never marry. There are several grades of priestly vocation: A monsignor performs special duties in a Catholic community; a bishop takes care of a diocese, the Catholic community in a city; an archbishop serves a large city; and a cardinal is an archbishop appointed by the pope as an advisor. One of the most significant functions of cardinals is to elect a new pope.

Designed by the Erasmo Calvani, the Santuario de la Virgen de Coromoto in Guanare is alleged to be the site where the Virgin appeared before the chief of the Cospes Indians in 1652.

THE CULT OF MARÍA LIONZA

María Lionza is the goddess of nature and fertility, and protector of forests, wild animals, and mineral wealth. She is worshiped by cult groups from all social classes in Venezuela, although she is particularly popular among the urban poor. The cult of María Lionza originated from Indian, African, and Christian beliefs and practices. She has the characteristics of an Arawak water goddess, West African mythological figures, and the Virgin Mary.

Legend has it that María Lionza was a beautiful Indian girl who disappeared in the forest and was never seen again, except as a spirit. She is said to live with her servants in a golden palace surrounded by wild animals in the Sorte Mountains of Yaracuy. She rides on the back of a tapir, a gentle beast considered sacred by some Indian groups.

During cult services, a priest calls up the spirits, and the spirits possess mediums. The spirits are consulted for advice and assistance. Tobacco smoke is used as a cure, to ward off evil spirits, and to bring about spiritual cleansing.

María Lionza has been associated with popular Catholic saints, with a historical figure named Negro Miguel who instigated an uprising among the slaves, and even with Simón Bolívar, the Venezuelan liberator. In the Sorte Mountains, there are countless images of the goddess. In ceremonies that take place in the mountains, candles burn everywhere and worshipers often go barefoot to maintain physical contact with the earth. They never stand with arms or hands crossed, as this is said to bring bad luck.

The worship of María Lionza takes many different forms throughout the country. An attempt was made to unify the cult groups in 1968, when they were legalized as a society under the name of the Aboriginal Cult of María Lionza, with its headquarters in Caracas.

ATTITUDES TOWARD CATHOLICISM

Although most Venezuelans consider themselves Catholic, religion does not play a significant role in daily life for all of them. Of the entire population, 96 percent are nominally Catholic, but only 25 percent practice their faith. Generally only the elderly attend Mass daily and pray before meals. Most of the younger Catholics attend Mass only on festive religious occasions such as Christmas, weddings, baptisms, and saints' days. For them, the social atmosphere often takes precedence over the religious significance of the ceremony.

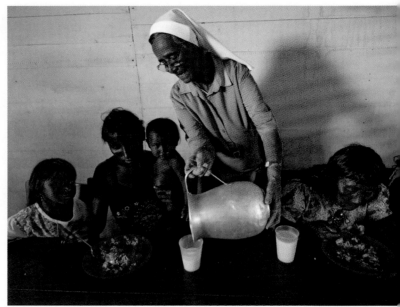

The Catholic Sisters in the convents work with poverty, infant mortality, and sanitation issues. They also feed the elderly and provide milk to malnourished babies.

The women tend to be more religious than the men, perhaps because they are responsible for the moral and religious education of their children. Boys are generally not encouraged to enter the religious life, because devotion is not considered a masculine trait. This may be why the Church has difficulty recruiting Venezuelan priests. Although about half the nuns in the country are local women, most priests in Venezuela come from Spain. Venezuelan priests usually come from the middle class, which has historically been more religious than the other classes.

Catholics in the rural states of Mérida, Táchira, and Trujillo, where agricultural traditions have been maintained, tend to be more devoted to their faith than Catholics in the cities. Perhaps the stresses of urban life leave little time for spiritual affairs; and perhaps the lure of the material world distracts sophisticated city folk from thoughts of life after death.

FOLK BELIEFS AND SUPERSTITIONS

Folk beliefs based on the occult are common throughout Venezuela, especially in remote rural areas. Folk beliefs combine Catholic beliefs and

This altar in the home of a family in the Miranda State pays homage to San Juan, also known as Saint John.

practices with those of African and Indian faiths. In the Andes some people believe that physical objects such as water contain supernatural powers. Venezuelans of all ethnic origins seek the advice of resident faith healers. Many indigenous Indians, especially among the Arawak and Carib, believe in the power of spiritualists.

Venezuelans are generally superstitious people. Many believe in witches and demons that take on human form and other spirits that take on animal forms. *Anima solas* (ah-NEE-mah SOH-lahs), or "lost souls," are said to make occasional appearances, and it is believed they are best diffused by covering one's face and praying aloud.

In Venezuela it is Tuesday the 13th rather than Friday the 13th that is considered unlucky. North American superstitions about walking under ladders and letting black cats cross your path are also heeded by Venezuelans. For good luck a polished seed of a tropical tree is as good as a rabbit's foot. The seed can be given as a gift, stolen, or found, but it must never be bought.

Some Venezuelans consider it bad luck to receive a handkerchief, seashell, live snake, or anything made from snakeskin. Others consider a rattlesnake tail to be a symbol of good luck. If the palm of your right hand itches, then someone owes you money; if the itch is in the left hand, then you owe someone money. When you open a bottle of rum, you are supposed to spill a few drops on the ground in order to give the dead a taste. If you dream about a snake, it means that someone is gossiping about you; if in the dream you behead the snake, this indicates that you have stopped the gossip from spreading.

OTHER RELIGIONS

Some other religions, such as the Baha'i and Protestant faiths, have experienced rapid growth in Venezuela in recent years, converting many Guajiro Indians. Judaism is represented in Venezuela by both Sephardic groups that came from Spain and Ashkenazi groups that emigrated from central and Eastern Europe after World War II.

Islam came to Venezuela first with African slaves and later with the waves of migrants from India and Pakistan (end of the 16th century), then Syria and Lebanon (middle of the 19th century), and continues with the influx of Middle Eastern immigrants under Chávez.

There are also several Greek and Ukrainian Orthodox congregations in Venezuela, as well as followers of Buddhism.

Catholics ask Saint Anthony for help when they are in need of special favors. Folk believers in rural Venezuela tie down a small statue of Saint Anthony until he grants them their request.

INTERNET LINKS

www.newadvent.org/cathen/15327a.htm

This site contains extremely detailed information on Venezuela's religious history.

www.caribeinsider.com/showreligion.do?code=002

This website provides detailed information on María Lionza from *Caribe Insider*.

http://venezuelanindian.blogspot.com/2008/08/maria-lionza-indigenous-myth-or-folk.html

This site includes information on María Lionza from a knowledgeable writer on Venezuela, Russell Maddick.

http://berkleycenter.georgetown.edu/resources/countries/venezuela

This site from the Berkley Center for Religion, Peace, and World Affairs contains information and links on religion in Venezuela.

LANGUAGE

A signboard in Venezuelan Spanish.

9

THE OFFICIAL language of Venezuela is Spanish, the language of the conquistadores. The standard of Spanish used among educated Venezuelans is uniform throughout the country, but the standard varies from region to region among the less educated.

People from the Andean states of Mérida, Trujillo, and Táchira speak with a refined accent. In Maracaibo people accentuate their syllables clearly, while the inhabitants of Cumaná and Margarita Island speak fast. The *llaneros* have a distinct accent, as do the inhabitants of Coro and Caracas. Nevertheless everyone understands everyone else.

Locals sharing a laugh in the park.

Anything typically Venezuelan is called criollo as a mark of its uniqueness to Venezuela. Venezuelan Spanish, despite its regional variations, is definitely criollo. As much as English has influenced Venezuelan Spanish and many locals have studied English and want to practice it, everyone in Venezuela is expected to speak Spanish, and the government is active in attempting to keep Venezuelan Spanish as "pure" as possible, ensuring all official communication is in Spanish. As an example, all government websites are available in Spanish only!

A dual language sign for a grocery store in Santo Domingo. Despite the pervasive influence of English, shop signs are all in Spanish.

"VENEZUELANISMS"

People of all classes and ethnic groups are familiar with many distinctly Venezuelan words. Some of these words come from several African and Indian languages, while others have Spanish origins.

Indian words that have found their way into the Venezuelan vocabulary include the Cumana-goto-derived *butaca* (boo-TAH-kah), meaning "theater stall;" and the Arawak-derived *hamaca* (ah-MAH-kah), meaning "hammock;" *barba-coa* (bar-bah-KOH-ah), meaning "barbecue;" and *tabaco* (ta-BAH-koh), meaning "tobacco." Some of these words were eventually Anglicized as well.

Some "Venezuelanisms" of Spanish origin have been adapted for use in modern situations. For example, in Caracas, a city renowned for traffic jams, *caraqueños* have devised a vocabulary to describe various types of congestion: a *galletas* (gah-YEH-taz) is your average traffic jam; *colas* (KOH-lahs) are long lines of traffic that crawl at snail's pace; and a *tranca* (TRAHN-cah) is a complete roadblock. *Vivos* (BEE-bohs) are drivers who pay no attention to traffic laws and thus often cause accidents.

AMERICAN INFLUENCE

Venezuelans who travel regularly or who come in contact with people from other cultures speak English as well as other languages, such as Portuguese, French, German, and Italian. There are also substantial immigrant populations whose first language is Portuguese or Italian.

English has been creeping steadily into the language, especially in urban areas, because of the influx of North Americans employed in the petroleum industry. In the areas of sports and recreation, the influence of the *yanqui*

(JAN-kee), or "yankee," is clear. For instance, in the national sport of baseball, called *beisbol* (beh-EES-bol) in Venezuela, "ball one" is *bol uán* (bol oo-WAN), "ball two" is *bol tu* (bol TOO), "strike three" is *estrai tri* (ess-TRAH-ee tree), "struck out" is *estrocao* (ess-troh-KAH-oh), "hit" is *hit* (heet), and "home run" is *jonrón* (khon-RHON). If these terms were translated directly into Spanish, they would not sound nearly as American.

Other Americanisms have been adopted in the office and beyond, such as "all right," or *olrai* (OHL-rah-ee). A security guard or night watchman is called a *wachiman* (wah-chih-MAHN), a clutch in a standard shift car is a *croche* (CROH-chay), and when your gas tank reads "F," it is *full* (fool).

Indians learning Spanish in a makeshift classroom in the middle of a forest.

A UNIFYING FORCE

Most Venezuelans speak only Spanish. This common language serves as a unifying base, contributing to the *Venezolano* sense of identity. Although there are distinct words to define the different ethnic groups, these terms do not carry racist connotations. A *blanco* (BLAHN-koh) is simply a Caucasian; a *negro* (NAY-groh) an African; a *mulatto* (moo-LAHT-toh) an African—Caucasian mix; a *pardo* (PAR-doh) someone of African, Caucasian, and Indian heritage; and a *zambo* (ZAHM-boh) an Indian—African mix. A mestizo, which used to refer to someone of Indian and European heritage, has come to designate all ethnic permutations.

INDIAN LANGUAGES

Before the conquistadores found Venezuela, the country was inhabited by culturally diverse groups of Indians. Historians speculate that there were four related groups of Indian languages in Venezuela before the Spanish arrived. These language groups were Cariban, Arawakan, Paezan, and Chib-chan. Many indigenous peoples in Venezuela—and their ancient languages—became extinct during the Spanish conquest. Linguists believe that just about 100 different languages and dialects are today spoken by Indians in Venezuela.

SPANISH NAMES

Many Venezuelans of Spanish heritage have double last names that can be confusing. If a man's name is Pedro Jimenez Garcia, he is called Señor Jimenez. Jimenez is his father's surname, and Garcia is his mother's maiden name. The latter distinguishes him from his cousins, who might be Emilio Jimenez Martinez or Jaime Jimenez Rodriquez.

If Pedro Jimenez Garcia marries Maria Estrada Gonzales, she becomes Maria Estrada de Jimenez or Señora de Jimenez. Estrada was her father's name and Gonzales her mother's maiden name, which is now dropped. Their children's surname will be Jimenez Estrada.

NOTIONS OF SPACE

Venezuelans, like other Latin Americans, are warm, demonstrative people: They tend to communicate a lot through body language and stand close to one another when conversing. While North Americans typically stand around

Teenage boys sharing a joke in a village in Venezuela.

ADDRESSES AND STREET NAMES IN CARACAS

Downtown Caracas is laid out on a grid, with streets running either parallel to or at right angles to each other, with a main north—south street. Parallel streets are identified by numbers, while streets laid out in an east—west direction have names. Many addresses are stated as intersections. For example *Hoyo a Santa Rosalía* designates the intersection of Hoyo and Santa Rosalía streets.

Corners derive their names from nearby buildings, well-known people who lived on them, or events that took place on them. For example, in Plaza Bolívar, the southeastern corner is called Las Gradillas, or "The Stairs," because at one time, a flight of steps led into the square at that spot. On the south side is a corner called Las Monjas, or "The Nuns," a name derived from an 18th-century convent that used to stand there. The convent was said to have been founded by a rich woman who encouraged the female members of her family to become nuns. There were once 70 nuns living in the convent. The building was demolished in 1874.

Caracas has five corners named after La Virgen del Carmen, or Our Lady of Mount Carmel. The best known of these, near Plaza Miranda, is called El Carmen, because of an image of Virgin Mary carved in relief on the facade of a building that once stood there.

There are many other examples of street corners named in similar fashion: One is called Pelota after a game that was once played there; another is called Hospital for a hospital that once stood there. Some are named after figures who were once well known in that area. The Marquis of Mija-res lived on the corner called Mijares, and the street corner Diaz is named after Dr. Diaz.

20 inches (51 cm) apart, Latin Americans keep a much smaller distance between themselves. This may make many North Americans feel uncomfortable, but it is considered unfriendly or cold to back away.

At formal meetings Venezuelans do not like facing each other across a table. Foreigners working in Venezuela are thus urged to furnish their offices with a sofa, or comfortable chairs placed arm to arm, so that participants in a business discussion can sit next to each other. Talking across a table can make Venezuelans feel uncomfortable or even snubbed.

Venezuelans tend to touch each other often. When introduced, two people shake hands. By the second meeting, new acquaintances are likely to embrace or pat each other on the right shoulder. This custom, the *abrazo* (ah-BRAH-soh), is done by both men and women. The shoulder pat is also used to comfort another person or when enjoying a good joke. Men and women who are good friends kiss each other to say hello and good-bye, as do women friends. Women often walk arm-in-arm in public.

At a party it is important to shake hands with each guest upon arriving and before leaving, and to look a person in the eye when speaking.

INTERNET LINKS

www.ethnologue.com/show_country.asp?name=VE

This site contains a comprehensive list of the languages of Venezuela.

www.aupairinamerica.com/resources/kids/culture_corner/ venezuela.asp

This website has links to Spanish language interactive activities.

http://quizlet.com/2282454/51010-cubanismos-ecuatorianismos-y- venezolanismos-flash-cards/

On this site you can find practice interactive exercises for Venezuelan and Latin expressions.

The stained glass, colored wall is a beautiful sight for all at the Caracas International Airport.

10

VENEZUELANS HAVE A LONG history of achievements in poetry, music, painting, and oratory. They are also well known for their Indian pottery, basketry, and weaving.

Caracas is the cultural and artistic center of the country. It is the home of museums and art galleries, including the Museo de Arte Contemporáneo (Museum of Contemporary Art), Galería de Arte Nacional (National Art Gallery), and Museo de Bellas Artes (Museum of Fine Arts), which specialize in works by both Venezuelan and foreign artists. The Venezuelan Symphony Orchestra offers concerts ranging from the classical to the modern; it even plays occasionally at subway stations during rush hour as part of the Metro's cultural program. Caracas has an accomplished ballet troupe, a national opera company, and several smaller musical ensembles. Architecturally the city has earned a reputation for innovation and imagination, especially through the buildings designed by the country's most famous architect, Carlos Raúl Villanueva.

Colonial homes have been painstakingly restored. The Museo de Arte Colonial (Museum of Colonial Art), a splendid 18th-century country residence, provides a glimpse of the lifestyle of a wealthy colonial family. In Spanish tradition the main house is surrounded by walls and encloses a patio. The rooms are filled with period furniture, paintings, and religious artifacts, and the balconies look out over a garden filled with indigenous orchids. A bathroom in a separate building has a large stone tub into which fresh spring water used to run. Kitchens, storerooms, and stables have been stocked with period utensils, tools, and carriages.

Venezuelan art provides yet another example of life being lived out in the open and the apparent contrasts of formal and informal, and modern blending with the traditional. In Caracas modern kinetic sculptures dot the landscape, as do the revolutionary murals created by groups expressing their political allegiance, including striking images such as Caravaggio's *David with the Head of Goliath*, in which Goliath is replaced by a representative of the Goliath of the United States, Hillary Clinton.

The interior of the "Black Cube" building in Caracas. Venezuelan op and kinetic artist, sculptor, and painter, Jesús Rafael Soto's creations are multi-dimensional and use a variety of materials such as plastic and steel.

CULTURAL HISTORY

During the colonial period it was the Catholic Church that was primarily responsible for encouraging cultural development. Venezuela's scholars and intellectuals were educated in religious schools, and their thoughts and writings reflected their religious background. At the same time the Church was also a great patron of the visual arts: It commissioned paintings and sculptures of religious events and figures for the numerous churches and cathedrals in the country.

In the 18th century the first portrait paintings began to appear in Venezuela, and in about 1784 the first plays were produced in Caracas' first theater. During the last years of the colonial era, the country was known throughout the Spanish empire for the brilliance of its composers and musicians.

Simón Bolívar was the leading intellectual icon of the independence movement. He had extraordinary oratorical abilities and his literary work is still considered to be among the country's finest prose. His tutor, Andrés Bello, a poet and philosopher, wrote the first book ever printed in Venezuela. He left the country with Bolívar in 1810 and eventually settled in Chile, where he helped develop the national education system.

During the independence era painting became increasingly important, as subject matter turned toward the political and the historical. Juan Lovera, a self-taught artist, is famous for his group portraits of the leaders of the movement. After independence artists rejected the Church's cultural hold and turned to events of the immediate past for inspiration, although they kept their European roots in terms of style. Poets such as José Antonio Martin and Abigaíl Lozano were popular during this time, as was Fermin Toro, who wrote some of Venezuela's first novels.

From 1870 to 1888, during the reign of the dictator Antonio Guzmán Blanco, Venezuela became culturally more sophisticated. A great admirer and patron of the arts, Guzmán Blanco built the Municipal Theater and the first Academy of Fine Arts, and appointed French romantic painter Martín Tovary Tovar, later known as the master of Venezuelan mural painting, as his official artist. Tovary Tovar's follower, Arturo Michelena, became one of South America's best-known painters.

Juan Vicente Gómez, a dictator who ruled Venezuela from 1908 to 1935, despised artists and intellectuals, and his reign inspired some of the country's finest political protest writing. Short-story writer Rufino Blanco Fombona was known for his satiric attacks on Gómez and his followers.

At Casa Natal, the birthplace of Simón Bolívar, visitors can see the family bed and Bolívar's library and files.

Other early-20th-century writers who helped define the Venezuelan artistic style include Teresa de las Parra, an upper-class woman who wrote an intimate novel about the effects of industrialization on the life of a *criollo* woman. Romantic poetry written in traditional Spanish couplets was also popular during this period. The leader of the cultural movement, Andrés Eloy Blanco, was known for his lighthearted style and his use of well-known Venezuelan proverbs and myths.

One of Venezuela's leading painters during the early 20th century was Armando Reverón. He spent much of his life in the small coastal town of Macuto, where he took advantage of the sunny Caribbean climate to depict selected models and landscapes. For example he created perhaps more than a hundred paintings of a small bay by his house, trying to capture the different shades of light produced at different times of the day.

MODERN TRENDS

With democracy and economic prosperity following the oil boom, public interest in art increased substantially. The government began assigning funds to ambitious artistic establishments such as the national symphony and filmmaking and ballet companies. Venezuelan artists were exposed to the work of artists from other cultures, especially Europe and the United States, and this had a significant impact on local art. At the same time, interest in indigenous folk art revived.

LITERATURE Historical fiction continues to appeal to many Venezuelans. Homegrown authors such as Arturo Uslar Pietri and Miguel Otero Silva have written greatly admired novels about the Spanish conquest and 20th-century dictators in Venezuela. In 1980 Luis Brito García won great acclaim with *Abrapalabra*, an experimental historical novel that was awarded a coveted literary prize—the National Prize for Literature. The average young Venezuelan prefers the novels of Francisco Herrera Luque, which give simpler, more colorful accounts of recent historical events. His *Boves el Urogallo*, about the war of independence, sold more copies than any other novel in Venezuelan history.

DANCE, MUSIC, THEATER In 1974 the national ballet company was established with dancers from all over the world. Ballet International de

A folk dance group preparing for the parade at the annual Feria de la Chinita in Maracaibo.

RÓMULO GALLEGOS AND *DOÑA BÁRBARA*

Venezuela's most famous novel, published in 1929, is Doña Bárbara by Rómulo Gallegos. Translated into many languages, the novel is considered the finest example of what is known as criollo literature, work that is truly Venezuelan in theme and tone. Like much of Gallegos's work, Doña Bárbara addresses the theme of the intellectual who struggles to civilize corrupt and violent elements in Venezuelan society.

The book's hero, Santo Luzardo, represents the civilizing force; Doña Bárbara, the primary female character, represents the barbaric force. The novel is set on the llanos, described as "a wide and stretching land, all horizons like hope, all roads like the will."

Doña Bárbara is the beautiful and imperious leader of the llaneros. During her youth her fiancé was killed and she was raped by a group of adventurers. From that point on she despised men and vowed to dominate them. Now at the height of her power, she wields control over all the men of the llanos—peons, butlers, landowners, and judges. She is skillful with both knife and gun and orders assassinations without a thought.

In the end, however, Santo Luzardo overcomes Doña Bárbara and her followers with the help of working-class llaneros. The moral of the story: Good always triumphs over evil.

Doña Bárbara brought Gallegos literary fame. The successful author later became a well-known politician. He served as director of the ministry of education in Caracas and became a member of both the senate and the house of deputies. In 1947 Gallegos was elected president, but was ousted by a military faction after only a few months in office. He died in 1969 at the age of 85.

Doña Bárbara was first made into a movie in 1943. Fernando de Fuentes wrote the screenplay and produced and directed his adaptation of Gallegos's novel. Then, in 1999, Betty Kaplan made her epic of the same title with a cast from Spain, Argentina, Cuba, and the United States.

Caracas toured Latin America and the United States in the late 1970s, performing the national dance, the *joropo* (ho-ROW-pow), to music provided by renowned Venezuelan pianist Teresa Carreño.

Venezuela's established musical groups—including the Maracaibo Symphony Orchestra founded in the early 1970s, the Caracas Opera Company, and the Venezuelan Symphony Orchestra—have achieved international recognition. Amateur and professional opera companies, choruses, and children's musical groups are popular locally.

In 2001 Caracas hosted its fifth Fiesta Internacional del Teatro San Martin, an annual international festival that brings together various professional, amateur, and alternative theater groups.

PAINTING AND SCULPTURE Venezuelan painters and sculptors have attracted attention in the international art world. The work of painter and sculptor Jesús Raphael Soto, in particular, is widely collected and displayed. Soto has held major exhibitions at the Hirshhorn Gallery in Washington, D.C., and the Guggenheim Museum in New York City.

The infamous statue of Venezuela's highest Santeria goddess, María Lionza, overlooks the Fajardo Highway in Caracas.

Born in Ciudad Bolívar in 1923, Soto studied in Caracas and Paris. His work is abstract, influenced by the Dutch painter Piet Mondrian and the American sculptor Alexander Calder. Many of Soto's pieces literally move, and he encourages viewers to see each piece from different perspectives. Soto founded a museum in Ciudad Bolívar that exhibits his own work as well as works of other contemporary artists from South America, the United States, and Europe.

Other well-known Venezuelan painters and sculptors include Alejandro Colina, Francisco Narvaes, and Alejandro Otero. Colina created the famous statue in Caracas of María Lionza riding her tapir; works by Narvaes and Otero grace many outdoor spaces in Venezuela.

ARCHITECTURE

Primarily through the work of Carlos Raúl Villanueva, Venezuela has become a bastion of architectural art. Educated in Paris, Villanueva returned to Caracas to found the College of Architecture at the Central University of Caracas. He supervised the construction of a housing project in one of the poorest neighborhoods of Caracas. Finished in 1943, El Silencio, as the project is known, was the first low-cost housing project to be constructed in Latin America on such a large scale.

Although Villanueva went on to design other similar projects, his finest work is thought to be the University City in Caracas. He stylized the structural layout of the campus with plazas, patios, gardens, and canopied walkways, and he commissioned other artists, such as Alexander Calder, Jean Arp, and Fernand Léger, to create murals and sculptures to further embellish the university landscape.

Villanueva also designed the Olympic Stadium and Olympic Pool, the Museum of Fine Arts, and the Maestranza César Girón bull ring in Maracay.

The Maracay bull ring built by President Juan Vicente Gómez was designed by Carlos Raúl Villanueva. It was Villanueva's first design project.

FOLK ARTS

Folk traditions in music, dance, and art have been of particular interest to Venezuelan youths since the early 1960s. Many traditional Venezuelan musical instruments that are played during holidays and religious festivals are Spanish in origin. The *cuatro* (KWAH-troh), or four-stringed guitar, which sounds a little like a ukulele, is often played along with the maracas, while people dance the *joropo*, a rhythmic, fast step with many regional variations.

Other dances include the waltz, the merengue of Caribbean origin, and a version of the Argentine tango called the *tanguito* (tahn-goo-WEE-toh). Percussion instruments of African origin may accompany Spanish songs, such as *tono* (TOH-noh) *llanero*, which is sung by the cowboys.

Cuatros for sale at a souvenir shop in Venezuela.

Indigenous Indians in Venezuela, especially the more isolated groups south of the Orinoco River, have a special chant for religious events. They also play a flute and a percussion instrument called a *culo en tierro* (KOO-loh ehn tih-AIR-roh), which is half a coconut husk placed face down on the ground and used as a drum.

Indigenous Indian handicrafts are made either for personal use or for sale to tourists. The Guajiro Indians are especially well known for their ceramics and their hammocks, which come in two varieties: a tight weave, or *hamaca*, and a loose weave, or *chinchorro*. Guajiro women create bright-colored designs on large looms at home. They also weave intricately patterned shawls and bags. Guajiro men are famous for their belts and saddlebags. Typical colors are yellow, red, and blue or green.

The Warau Indians of the Orinoco Delta are known not only for hammocks, but also for delicate baskets woven from dyed palm fibers and intricate wooden figurines carved in the shape of animals, insects, birds, fish, snakes, and dolphins. Groups in the Amazonas Federal Territory, such as the Makiritare, Piaroa, and Yanomami, also make beautiful baskets, masks, blowpipes, feather and bead ornaments, rings from black stones, and carved hardwood stools. The mountain people of the Andes knit sweaters, woolen blankets, and ponchos called ruanas. *Llaneros* are known for rope-soled shoes, handmade leather goods such as lassos, and musical instruments such as the harp, *cuatro*, and maracas.

INTERNET LINKS

http://worldmusic.nationalgeographic.com/view/page.basic/country/content.country/venezuela_40

This site contains information on Venezuelan music stars.

http://carnaval.com/venezuela/music/

This website provides detailed information on different Venezuelan musical styles.

http://fiestajazz.com/articulo.html

This site takes visitors on a tour of the music found in different parts of Venezuela.

www.fmn.gob.ve

This website is for all major museums in Venezuela. It is available in Spanish only.

www.fundacionbigott.com

This site has information and publications on Venezuelan culture and traditions, including music from the Bigott Foundation.

http://globalvoicesonline.org/2011/03/23/venezuela-learning-to-play-the-cuatro-on-the-web-2-0/

This site includes a video tutorial on playing Venezuela's traditional four-string guitar.

LEISURE

A boy swinging a baseball bat in Caracas.

11

V ENEZUELAN LEISURE TIME is spent playing sports, watching television, listening to the radio, reading the newspaper, or simply chatting with friends over coffee. There are also national parks for contact with nature, museums for educational recreation, golf courses for relaxing exercise, and theaters and nightclubs for entertainment.

Traditional Venezuelans spend a lot of their leisure time at home with their family, celebrating birthdays and religious holidays or simply getting together on weekends. For recreation upper-class *caraqueños*, like urban North Americans, often go to shopping malls, to the movies, to cafés and restaurants, or to a private club.

In rural areas it is at the local grocery store that people congregate to relax and discuss the events of the day.

BASEBALL — THE NATIONAL SPORT

Baseball came to Venezuela from the United States in the 1890s. A group of upper-class Venezuelan students opened the first club in Caracas in 1895. Latin American countries that had the greatest enthusiasm for baseball—Cuba, Nicaragua, the Dominican Republic, Panama, Colombia, and Venezuela—felt a strong North American presence; countries where soccer predominated—Brazil, Argentina, Chile, Uruguay, and Peru— were more influenced by the Europeans.

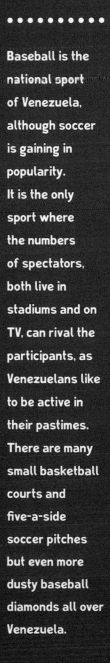

Baseball is the national sport of Venezuela, although soccer is gaining in popularity. It is the only sport where the numbers of spectators, both live in stadiums and on TV, can rival the participants, as Venezuelans like to be active in their pastimes. There are many small basketball courts and five-a-side soccer pitches but even more dusty baseball diamonds all over Venezuela.

The earliest Venezuelan baseball teams were made up of the sons of wealthy families living in an affluent suburb of Caracas called El Paraíso, where a baseball field was built in 1902. Soon people from all walks of life formed street teams, and the sport gained mass appeal. After 1918 teams began to be organized more professionally, and by 1949 the government had instituted a program to build baseball fields and stadiums all over the country.

The professional baseball season in Venezuela lasts from October to February. Some well-known North American major leaguers play in Venezuela during their off-season, while Venezuelan major leaguers hit fields in the United States between March and September.

Venezuelans have played for the Toronto Blue Jays, the New York Yankees, the Chicago Cubs and White Sox, and the Cincinnati Reds, among others. Famous Venezuelan major leaguers include Luis Sojo, Omar Vizquel, and Andrés "Big Cat" Galarraga. Magglio Ordóñez is one of Venezuela's biggest new-generation baseball stars.

Venezuelan baseball teams include the Caracas Lions, the Magallanes Navigators, the Zulia Eagles, the Aragua Tigers, and the Lara Cardinals.

LESSER SPORTS

Soccer, basketball, and boxing are also popular in Venezuela, at both amateur and professional levels. Volleyball games, wrestling matches, and automobile and bicycle races are also usually well attended.

In small towns people enjoy watching and betting on cockfights. A lot of money is wagered on these well-trained birds, even though their competitive careers can be over in a matter of minutes.

Betting on racehorses is another popular leisure activity. The bet, called the *cinco y seis* (SIN-koh ee SEYS), a kind of daily double, has become so popular that the phrase is used to describe any unlikely possibility. The Rinco-nada Hippodrome in Caracas is one of the most sophisticated tracks in Latin America. It has 2,000 stables and even a swimming pool for horses. On weekends 20,000 Venezuelans pack the grandstands to watch the races firsthand, while millions watch the races on television.

About 10 to 12 bullfights are held each year in Caracas, but most of the matadors come from abroad. Bullfights are also held in Maracay, Valencia, Mérida, and San Cristóbal. Rodeos, or *toros coleados* (TOH-rohs coh-lay-AH-dos), are held in small towns in the llanos.

Along the Caribbean coast, water sports such as deep-sea fishing, scuba diving, snorkeling, waterskiing, and sailing are quite popular.

OTHER AMUSEMENTS

For entertainment Venezuelans in the cities often attend cultural performances such as the ballet and symphony; many also go to the movies. Although Venezuela has its own filmmaking industry, most of the films screened in the theaters are imported from Europe and the United States and dubbed in Spanish.

Watching television is a common diversion for Venezuelans of all social classes. Television came to the country in 1952. Today there are five regular TV stations. Most Venezuelans have regular access to television; there are more than 4 million television sets currently in use. There are 171 TV sets per 1,000 people and 40 cable subscribers per 1,000 people. Among the lower classes, the television set is a status symbol; it is not uncommon to see television antennas on the roofs of the ranchos, or shanties, that crowd the outskirts of the urban areas.

Although Venezuela imports many television shows from the United States and other Latin American countries, it also provides news and entertainment in Spanish to Latin America, Spain, Portugal, and the growing Hispanic population in the United States. The state TV channel is Venezolana de Televisión, which features a regular program presenting the thoughts of

Hundreds of spectators in the stands at a bull fighting ring in Venezuela.

Baseball is to Venezuelans what soccer is to the British; it is the national obsession. Nearly every town in Venezuela has its own stadium and team. Fans cheer with gusto for their favorite players. Some 200,000 boys ages 5 to 18 play in amateur leagues.

Hugo Chávez, and there are also four privately owned TV networks, plus numerous cable channels. Venevision, the country's top television channel, reaches 8 million viewers around the world. It is mandatory for all networks to broadcast government announcements when required.

Soap operas, or *telenovelas* (tay-lay-noh-BAY-lahs), are extremely popular. Due to their adult content, they are broadcast at night, when children are asleep. Some Venezuelan *telenovelas* are exported to the United States for Latin American communities there.

Radio is also popular in Venezuela. In the late 1990s there were 201 AM stations and 20 FM stations in Caracas and nearly 11 million radios in the country. The government-owned Radio Nacional de Venezuela runs 65 news stations and 30 stations covering specific audiences, broadcasting mostly cultural and educational programs. There are also 244 state-sponsored community radio stations and 36 TV stations.

In 1999 there were 11 Internet service providers in Venezuela and 27.8 personal computers per 1,000 people. This number had grown to 46 PCs per 1,000 people in 2010, with 950,000 people having Internet access.

Both spectators and players enjoy chess in the outdoors of Venezuela.

LEISURE AND SOCIAL LIFE

The private club is the center of social activities for the upper classes. On Sundays upper-class families gather at the club to make use of the facilities: squash courts, swimming pools, restaurants, gyms, and spas. Some women also spend weekdays at the club with friends, either playing cards or having luncheons or tea parties. Men tend to gather at the club to drink, play dominoes or cards, or chat with friends.

In rural areas men gather at the general store on Sundays and in the evenings to drink beer or sugarcane alcohol and occasionally play lawn bowling. Other customers who enter the store at these times usually make their purchases promptly and leave.

In very poor areas social life is even more informal. People tend to chat with their neighbors while doing the household chores or sitting on the patio. More active socializing takes place during momentous occasions such as weddings, funerals, and religious festivals.

Telenovelas, also known as teleculebras, or television snakes, are often stories about the lives and loves of a group of not-too-likable people. A show called Pasionaria (Passionate) was a hit in Venezuela.

INTERNET LINKS

www.pressreference.com/Uz-Z/Venezuela.html

This site contains detailed information on the media in Venezuela.

www.bumblehood.com/article/HwEq3enMS5C6gbwkpna1jQ

This website provides information on the major sports in Venezuela.

http://sports.espn.go.com/mlb/worldclassic2006/news/story?id=2291228

This site includes detailed information on Venezuelan baseball.

http://iml.jou.ufl.edu/projects/fall02/landino/index.html

This is an attractive site on Venezuelan baseball, including player profiles.

FESTIVALS

Costumed Devil Dancers parade through the streets during the annual Corpus Christi Day celebration in San Francisco de Yare, Miranda State.

12

VENEZUELAN FESTIVALS, or fiestas, are usually religious, although some have political origins. All Venezuelans celebrate Christmas, Easter, and Independence Day, but some of the other holidays, such as patron saints' days, are celebrated only in certain towns or villages.

The same patron saint's day may be observed differently in different villages, although most celebrations include fireworks, processions, street dances, and games. Depending on the history of the town, festival customs can have an African, Spanish, or Indian flavor, or a blend of all three.

Festivals in Venezuela are often times for families to take a holiday. In the larger cities, holidays such as Holy Week—the week before Easter—have lost their religious significance and become occasions for families to go on a holiday. Many urban dwellers—and nearly all *caraqueños*—leave the city during Holy Week to travel abroad or to visit relatives in nearby states.

In many Andean towns, however, Holy Week is celebrated with great vigor: Passion plays are acted out, robed and hooded penitents go to Mass on their knees, and large images of Judas are burned in the town square.

In many rural areas religious festivals and patron saints' days provide the only real entertainment for farming families during the year. Festivities sponsored by local religious groups, merchants, or prominent citizens give people a chance to meet old friends and family members, watch cockfights, attend special Masses and elaborate processions, and dance, drink, and listen to music all night.

Venezuelans revel in their festivities, always looking keenly forward to one with considerable anticipation, and hoping to gain a *Puente* (bridge) to the weekend if a festival falls, for example, on a Thursday. This involves taking official or unofficial time off work, paid or unpaid. This would mean they have from Thursday to Sunday (or even Monday) to fully appreciate the experience.

CARNIVAL

In Caracas and some other towns, the principal fiesta is Carnival, a two-day celebration that takes place in either February or March on the Monday or Tuesday before Ash Wednesday. Carnival is the last festivity before the six-week period of Lent. People dress up in wild costumes, dance in the streets, and live a bit recklessly in anticipation of the weeks of personal sacrifice and religious contemplation that will follow. Most stores and businesses close during Carnival.

The festivities begin with a large parade, complete with elaborately decorated floats and people dressed in colorful costumes. Entire streets are roped off during the festival, so people can dance the *joropo* and other Venezuelan dances and sing traditional songs.

In Caracas water fights are common during Carnival, and people are known to decorate statues of Simón Bolívar with wreaths and flowers. In the town of El Callao in Bolívar State, calypso music of Caribbean origin is played, while in the German village of Colonia Tovar, a mock funeral is held to mark the end of the festivities.

Venezuelans celebrate Carnival, the colorful festival of indulgence that throws South America into joyful chaos before the fasting season of Lent.

CORPUS CHRISTI

This is probably the most colorful festival in Venezuela. Celebrated on the Thursday after Trinity Sunday, it takes place about nine weeks after Easter in the town of San Francisco de Yare in Miranda State and in some villages in the states of Aragua and Carabobo.

Legend has it that a humble nun, Saint Juliana, often had visions while praying. One day Christ appeared to her and indicated the meaning of her visions: the absence of a festival to honor the Blessed Sacrament. Thus the Festival of Corpus Christi began in honor of the Eucharist—the bread and wine Catholics believe transform into the body and blood of Christ when consecrated during Mass.

CALENDAR OF HOLIDAYS IN VENEZUELA

These are Venezuela's national holidays and festivals.

January 1	*New Year's Day*
February/March	*Two-day Carnival (below)*
	Ash Wednesday
March/April	*Holy Thursday*
	Good Friday
	Easter
April 19	*Declaration of Independence*
May 1	*Labor Day (often also Ascension and Corpus Christi Day)*
June 24	*Battle of Carabobo*
July 5	*Independence Day*
July 24	*Birth of Simón Bolívar*
October 12	*Columbus Day*
November 1	*All Saints' Day*
December 17	*Death of Simón Bolívar*
December 24	*Christmas Eve*
December 25	*Christmas Day*
December 31	*New Year's Eve*

Performers dressed as devils dance during a parade to celebrate the Catholic festival of Corpus Christi in Ocumare de la Costa in the central state of Aragua.

For the famous festival that takes place in San Francisco de Yare, people dress up in baggy red costumes with crosses pinned to them, carry rosaries, and wear papier-mâché horned masks that resemble frightening bulls' heads. They are called the Devil Dancers.

At 6:00 A.M. on the morning of the festival, the dancers gather in front of the village church and dance vigorously to the beat of Venezuelan music. They attend Mass in the church and then return to their dancing, which by now has become even fiercer. Afterward they visit the homes of important people in the village, who give them money or liquor.

In the afternoon another procession forms near the church; each time it approaches the Devil Dancers, the members of the procession recoil in fear. Finally everyone returns to the church, where the Devil Dancers take off their masks and receive Holy Communion.

It is believed that the dancing and musical styles used during the celebration of Corpus Christi in San Francisco de Yare derive directly from non-Christian rituals practiced by the Ayoman Indians who used to inhabit the region.

CHRISTMAS IN VENEZUELA

The celebration of Christmas in Venezuela has undergone rather drastic changes in recent years. In the old days people used to set up a *nacimiento* (nah-sih-mih-EHN-toh), or nativity scene, in the patio or living room of their home. The *nacimiento* contained small carved images of the holy family, the wise men, shepherds and sheep, stable animals, and a star. The background had houses, lakes, and roads, and the whole scene was placed on folded cloth resembling mountains.

Passersby would admire the *nacimiento* through the windows of the living room, and the family would gather there in the evening to sing carols or recount the Christmas story. The figure of the baby Jesus was placed in the manger only on Christmas Eve, and the figures of the Three Kings were situated far from the child and moved up a little bit every day until they reached him on January 6, the Epiphany.

In the past Venezuelan children did not know Santa Claus; they got their gifts from the Three Kings, and they opened their presents on Epiphany, rather than on Christmas. The children would place their shoes under their beds on the night of January 5, and in the morning, they would find their shoes filled with small toys, fruits, and other treats.

Christmas illumination of Avenida Bella Vista in Maracaibo, Zulia.

It was also a tradition to begin attending Christmas Mass as early as December 16, at 4:00 A.M.! After Mass churchgoers would be met by groups singing carols and playing maracas; then they would drink the traditional after-Mass cup of sweetened black coffee and munch on a crispy corn fritter called a *masa* (MAH-sah), which could be purchased from a woman frying the fritters on a small grill by the road.

More recently Venezuelans celebrating Christmas, especially young people, roller-skate in the village plaza all night long, indulge in hot chocolate and long fried doughnuts in the shape of twisted ropes, and then attend Mass at dawn.

These traditions still take place in some areas, but they are dying out. The typical Venezuelan Christmas is now much like the typical North American Christmas. Gifts from Santa Claus rather than the Three Kings are wrapped in festive paper and placed under the Christmas tree to be opened on Christmas morning.

One Venezuelan Christmas tradition that has not been lost, however, is the inclusion of music in the celebration. Young people train for months to compete in Christmas music competitions in which *gaitas* (GAY-tahs), or bands playing traditional Venezuelan instruments, attempt to outperform

Venezuelan folk musicians playing at a festival.

one another. *Gaita* instruments usually consist of a four-stringed guitar, or cuatro, a common drum, maracas, and an unusual percussion instrument called a *furruco* (foo-ROO-koh). This is a drum with a hole in the center into which a long stick is inserted and rubbed up and down to create a hoarse, resonant sound.

Gaitas move from house to house on Christmas day, especially in Caracas, playing traditional music and accompanied by choruses singing Venezuelan songs.

PATRON SAINTS' DAYS

Nearly every Venezuelan village has a patron saint and an annual festival held in the saint's honor. It is customary to carry images of the patron saint through the streets in formal procession, after which dances, bullfights, competitions, and rodeos take center stage.

East of Caracas, in the village of Guatire, celebrants honor Saint Peter by blackening their faces and donning top hats. Saint Peter used to be invoked throughout the Christian world against fever because, according to the Bible, Christ cured Saint Peter's mother-in-law of a fever. Legend in Guatire has it that a slave woman's child was cured through her prayers to Saint Peter, and she danced all day to offer her thanks to the saint. Saint Peter's Day is thus celebrated with dancing somewhat resembling that of the Devil Dancers on Corpus Christi.

The festival of Saint John is celebrated primarily on the Caribbean coast in Miranda State, which has a large African population. This festival has elements that are distinctly African in origin. The framework of the fiesta is Spanish, but the music that accompanies the dancing is played on African drums. The festival is associated with the summer festivals of pre-Christian times, where fires were lit to greet the beginning of summer, and celebrants gathered around and jumped through the fires and sang traditional songs praising both saint and season. Taking place from June 23 through June 25, the festival of Saint John is remarkable for its unrelenting street dancing.

The festival of Saint Benito, or Saint Benedict, on December 27 also has a strong African heritage, although it is now celebrated by Venezuelans of all ethnic groups. In the area near Lake Maracaibo, Saint Benito is honored differently from village to village. The Paruajano Indians of Sinamaica Lagoon place images of the saint in boats and sail to a designated area where a special altar has been erected to honor him. Then the drumming starts and the villagers take turns dancing with images of the saint. In El Mojan, which is very close to the lagoon, criollo celebrants carry saint figures through the streets, dancing an entirely different step to the music of the cuatro and different drums.

In Gibraltar and Bobures, African people celebrate with yet another form of dancing that is distinctly African in tempo. In Timotes, in Mérida State, dancers carry maracas, blacken their faces with paint, and wear black grass skirts and feathered head-dresses. Others don the traditional Venezuelan *liqui-liqui* or wear a cowboy-like costume with a red fringe.

Devotees carrying the figure of San Juan, or Saint John.

INTERNET LINKS

www.thehistoryofchristmas.com/traditions/venezuela.htm
This site describes Christmas traditions in Venezuela.

www.123newyear.com/newyear-traditions/new-year-traditions-venezuela.html
This site explains New Year traditions in Venezuela.

www.carnaval.com/main.htm
This website contains extensive information and images of Venezuelan festivals.

Venezuelan festivals, especially the saints' days, are a distillation of the culture of that particular part of the country, often featuring unique music, food, dance, and customs.

FOOD

One interesting fish consumed by many Venezuelans is the colorful pirana fish, found mainly in the Orinoco Delta.

13

THE CUISINE OF VENEZUELA—like its customs and traditions, religious rituals, and language—shows Indian, Spanish, and African influences. Many staples of the Venezuelan diet were cultivated by the Indians in precolonial days, and many ingredients commonly used in local dishes originally came from Spain and Africa during the colonial period.

The early Indians of South America cultivated corn, beans, and squash. Upon their arrival in the New World, the Spanish conquistadores found other foods such as avocados, Brazil nuts, chocolate, guavas, manioc (bitter cassava), papayas, passion fruit, pineapples, and tomatoes.

While the conquistadores brought many of these foods back to Spain, they also brought chickens, pigs, garlic, onions, olive oil, rice, garbanzo beans, or chickpeas, and sugarcane to South America. Two Spanish-derived dishes are Spanish omelette—chickpea flour batter over boiled potato slices and broccoli florets—and Spanish rice—white rice fried with onions, red peppers, carrots, and other vegetables.

Coffee, the most beloved drink of South America, originated in Ethiopia and made its way to South America via the Middle East. Bananas and plantains, which are very much a part of the Venezuelan diet, came to the New World from Africa and the Canary Islands, although they originated in India and Malaysia.

Many of the ingredients brought from the outside world were readily accepted into the Venezuelan diet. Over the years, they were adapted to

Venezuelans eat in all kinds of food outlets in a variety of ways, depending on time and appetite— at home, in restaurants, cafés, from kiosks or street stalls. Street food varies from a bag of chips or an ice cream to *cachitos* (similar to croissants) with ham and cheese, *hallacas* at Christmas, *arepas* and empanadas, and hot dogs, all the way up to a burger constructed with beef patties, avocado, a fried egg, bacon, cheese, and the sauces of your choice!

In the old days women in rural villages made arepas *by heating corn kernels and water over a fire. The ingredients were brought to a boil, but it was essential not to let them actually boil, or the resulting dough would be thick and lumpy. The mixture was left to cool overnight. In the morning, the corn was drained into a basket and carried to the river where it was dunked over and over until the corn hulls loosened and floated away.*

The soft corn kernels that remained were placed into a grinder and made into corn dough called masa. *For breakfast people used to fry a fresh* arepa, *put a little butter or grated white cheese on it, and eat it with their coffee and milk.*

Arepas being served at that state-run Arepa Socialista restaurant in Caracas—an initiative to nourish stomachs and souls with a subsidized version of the beloved dish.

suit the criollo palate, and what emerged was a cuisine that, while sharing some cooking traditions with other Latin American cultures, was in many ways unique to Venezuela. This cuisine, called *comida criolla,* is based essentially on pancakes, soups and stews, and meats such as chicken, pork, and beef. Cheap set meals served in some restaurants in Venezuela usually include a soup with the main course.

SPECIALTIES

AREPA (ah-RAY-pah) Of Indian origin, this staple of the Venezuelan diet resembles a very thick Mexican tortilla. It is made by mixing either yellow or white corn flour with salt and enough water to make a dough. After being formed into a ball or patty, the *arepa* is toasted on a griddle, wrapped in a napkin, and served in a straw basket. To enhance its flavor, the *arepa* may be stuffed with ground beef, cheese, avocado, tuna, ham, eggs, beans, shrimp, and even shark. Eaten on its own, the *arepa* is almost tasteless; the stuffed *arepas,* however, are delicious.

Caraqueños often eat *arepas* in restaurants called *areperas* (ah-ray-PAIR-rahs) rather than at home, although prepared *arepa* flour is available in grocery stores.

SOPA DE FRIJOLES NEGROS (BLACK BEAN SOUP)

This recipe makes enough soup for six.

1 pound (450 g) black beans

1 chopped medium onion

2 cloves garlic, chopped

½ teaspoon (2.5 ml) cumin

1 teaspoon (5 ml) hot red chili, dried and crumbled

6 cups (1.5 L) beef stock

Salt to taste

1 chopped hard-boiled egg (optional)

Rinse the beans and soak them overnight. When ready to cook, drain the beans and rinse again. Place the beans in a large saucepan. Add the beef stock, chopped onion and garlic, cumin, and chili. Cover and simmer over low heat for about 2½ hours, until the beans are very soft. (The time will vary, depending on the age of the beans.) Puree the beans in a food processor, adding some of the beef stock. (Puree in batches, if necessary.) Pour the puree into the saucepan. Season with salt and heat through. Serve garnished with chopped hard-boiled egg, if you like.

BLACK BEANS Black beans are a popular item on the Venezuelan menu across economic and social classes. The main ingredients in the national dish, *pabellon* (pah-beh-YON) *criollo*, are stewed shredded meat, rice, and black beans, topped with sautéed bananas. *Pabellon criollo* is based on a 16th-century Spanish recipe called *ropa vieja* (ROH-pah bih-EH-hah), which means "old clothes." Many Venezuelans say that no restaurant could possibly prepare good *pabellon criollo*; this dish has to be prepared at home, according to secret family recipes.

Traditionally eaten on Christmas Eve, *hallacas* are very popular with Venezuelans.

HALLACA A dish that unifies the national cuisine is the *hallaca* (ah-YAH-kah). Traditionally made during Christmas, the *hallaca* is the dish that Venezuelans yearn for when they are away from home. They say one can cook the *hallaca* properly only after years of practice and with the help of the whole family. Invented by the Indians in precolonial days, *hallacas* are essentially little corn dough pies filled with meat, chicken, or other ingredients, wrapped inside a banana leaf in a flat rectangle, and boiled. The banana leaf seals in and enhances the flavor of the *hallaca*. Different regions add their own special touches: eggs, olives, raisins, or vegetables. But, no matter what the ingredients, a platter of *hallacas* occupies the seat of honor on the Christmas Eve dining table.

DESSERTS

Several Venezuelan dishes are made using coconut or coconut milk: rice dishes, meat stews and soups, and especially desserts. A famous Venezuelan cake, *bien me sabe de coco* (bih-ehn may SAH-bay day KOH-koh), is made by moistening plain cake with muscatel wine and coconut cream. Coconut is also used in candies or combined with caramel to make what is called a *coquito* (koh-KIH-toh).

Flan, a type of Spanish pudding of baked egg custard with a caramel topping, is also served for dessert as are a wide variety of tropical fruits such as mango, guava, pineapple, and papaya.

COFFEE

South Americans are great coffee drinkers. They drink a cup at each meal and several times in between meals. Friends often meet each other in the street and go to a café or a little outdoor coffee stand to indulge in a cup of coffee and some satisfying gossip.

Although about half the world's coffee is now grown in Latin America, the plant itself originally came from Africa. From there it traveled to the Arab nations, where it became an acceptable stimulant for Muslims, who are forbidden to drink alcohol. Coffee arrived in Europe with the Turkish invaders in the early 1600s, and in Latin America in the 1720s. Brazil and Colombia are famous for their excellent coffee, and the Venezuelan crop, though small, is reasonably good. In fact, Venezuela produces the famous *café azul de Caracas* (KAH-fay ah-ZOOL day kah-RAH-kass), or the blue coffee bean of Caracas, which is of very high quality.

Coffee is so popular in Venezuela that the drink has a vocabulary of its own: *café con leche* (KAH-fay kon LEH-chay) is coffee with hot milk; a large cup of mild black coffee is called a *guayoyo* (goo-ay-YOH-yoh); a *negro* (NAY-groh) is a large cup of strong black coffee; a *negrito* (nay-GRIH-toh) is a small cup or demitasse of strong black coffee; a *cafecito* (kah-fay-SIH-toh) is a demitasse of sweetened coffee; a large cup of strong coffee with a little milk added is called a *marron* (mah-ROHN); and a demitasse of strong coffee with a little milk added is called a *marroncito* (mah-rahn-SIH-toh).

Coffee beans drying in the courtyard in Los Altos de Sucre.

EATING OUT

Men in a barbecue kiosk on Margarita Island preparing sausages, chicken, pork, and beef chops.

Caraqueños eat out regularly and often. Whether they opt for a pizza parlor, a fast-food outlet, or a famous French restaurant in an elegant hotel, *caraqueños* have a wide variety of places at which to eat. The most popular places include criollo restaurants specializing in local cuisine, pasta places, *areperas* that are often open all night, steak houses specializing in Argentine cuisine, and Spanish restaurants where *tascas* (TAHS-cahs), or grilled seafood snacks, are offered and dining is accompanied by Spanish music.

Restaurateurs use ingredients that are grown only in Venezuela for some recipes: rice from Guárico State, tomatoes and miniature peppers from Margarita Island, freshwater prawns and lobsters from the Caribbean, beef from the llanos. After dinner many young people like to spend time in piano bars or cafés, enjoying coffee, fresh fruit shakes, and desserts.

Caracas has the most sophisticated international cuisine, but many states have famous dishes of their own: Zulia is known for fish from Lake Maracaibo and plantains; Trujillo for pastries and braised chicken; Mérida for dishes made from local chickpeas and green peas; Falcón for goat's meat recipes and cheese and fudge made from goat's milk; Bolívar for fish stews; the Caribbean states for an array of fresh seafood dishes including *pargo* (PAR-goh), or red snapper; and Táchira for chicken soup made with milk and hot peppers.

EATING AT HOME

The typical Caracas family wakes up for breakfast at 6:00 A.M., so the children can be in school by 7:00 A.M. Standard breakfast fare includes eggs, *arepas*, bread or rolls, fresh fruit juice, and coffee. Lunch is served from noon to 2:00

P.M. and is the most important meal of the day. A typical lunch consists of soup, salad, meat and vegetables, fruit, and dessert, which is often a pastry or tart. Water, soft drink, beer, or lemonade washes down the meal.

Dinner is usually a light meal, and it is served late, at about 9:00 P.M. *Arepas*, soup, and a sandwich or eggs are typical dinner fare. Some Venezuelans have hot chocolate before bed or at breakfast. Men drink whiskey, beer, rum, or wine at the cocktail hour; women rarely consume alcohol.

Although lunch is the most significant meal of the day for families in Venezuela, dinner is the meal most associated with entertaining. Some dinner parties begin as late as 11:00 P.M., and do not end until 3:00 A.M. or later. Even if a dinner begins early, it can end as late as midnight. The wife and husband usually sit at the head and foot of the table, with the guest of honor seated next to one or the other.

At upper-class gatherings, the food is served by a maid, and guests are not permitted to start eating until everyone at the table has been served. When hosting a dinner party, Venezuelans do not push their guests to finish everything on their plates or to have additional helpings. When the guests have had their fill, they often place the knife and fork together on the plate in such a manner as to resemble "ten o'clock" on a timepiece.

Aside from the home favorites, Caracas and major cities in Venezuela have a wide variety of ethnic restaurants that serve Arab, Chinese, Japanese, Hungarian, Portuguese, Colombian, Mexican, Trinidadian, Cuban, Swiss, and German food.

INTERNET LINKS

www.venezuelanfoodanddrinks.blogspot.com/2009/05/guayoyo-o-tetero-flaco-venezuelan.html

This site contains a glossary of Venezuelan terms for coffee.

www.southamerica.cl/Venezuela/Food.htm

This website provides information on typical Venezuelan food (and the foods of other Latin American countries).

www.recipes4us.co.uk/Venezuelan%20Recipes.htm

This site contains lots of Venezuelan recipes to try.

ROPA VIEJA AL ESTILO VENEZOLANO (SHREDDED BEEF)

This recipe serves six.

2 pounds (900 g) flank steak in one piece

2 cups (500 ml) beef stock

3 tablespoons (45 ml) corn oil

1 chopped onion

2 cloves garlic, chopped

2 sweet red peppers, seeded and chopped

Pinch of cumin

1 teaspoon (5 ml) hot paprika or hot sauce

Salt

Freshly ground pepper

Place the beef into a flameproof casserole and pour in enough stock to cover it. Bring to a simmer, cover and cook over low heat until it is tender, for about 2 hours. Cool in the stock. Remove the beef and shred it. Cover and set aside. Reserve the stock. Heat the oil in a large frying pan and sauté the onion, garlic, and red peppers until they are soft. Add the tomatoes, cumin, paprika, salt, and pepper and cook for 5 minutes longer, until the mixture is thick and well blended. Stir in the reserved shredded beef and about half a cup of the stock and simmer for 5 minutes longer to blend the flavors. Taste for seasoning and add more hot paprika, if desired. Serve with rice or bread.

AREPAS (CORN CAKES)

This recipe makes five *arepas*.

2 cups (500 ml) water

2 teaspoons (10 ml) salt

1 teaspoon (5 ml) cooking oil

2 cups (500 ml) finely ground,
   pre-cooked cornmeal (preferably white)

Butter and cheese (optional)

Pour the water into a large bowl and add the salt and cooking oil. Slowly add the cornmeal, and knead into a dough. (Cheese may be mixed in to add flavor to the dough.) Pat a small amount of the dough into a flat, round cake about ¼ inch (roughly 6 millimeters) thick. Smooth the edges of the cake. Make as many cakes as needed to use up the dough. Heat a greased skillet or griddle over a low flame. Place the cakes on the griddle, a few at a time, to brown on both sides. Then place them in the oven to bake for about 15 minutes. To serve, slice each *arepa* as you would a hamburger bun, remove a little of the soft steaming meal from the middle, stuff with desired filling, and close the *arepa*. Alternatively make the *arepas* about the size of a dollar coin and fry in oil until golden brown on both sides. Serve as bread with butter and cheese.

ARROZ CON LECHE (RICE WITH MILK)

12 tablespoons (180 ml) rice

1 cup (250 ml) water

4 cups (1 L) milk

6 tablespoons (90 ml) sugar

1 cinnamon stick

Powdered cinnamon (optional)

Wash rice thoroughly and place in water over a hot stove. When the water has evaporated, add milk and cinnamon stick. Cook over low heat to a creamy consistency. Add sugar and salt. Cook until thick, constantly stirring. Remove from fire. When a little cooler, sprinkle powdered cinnamon.

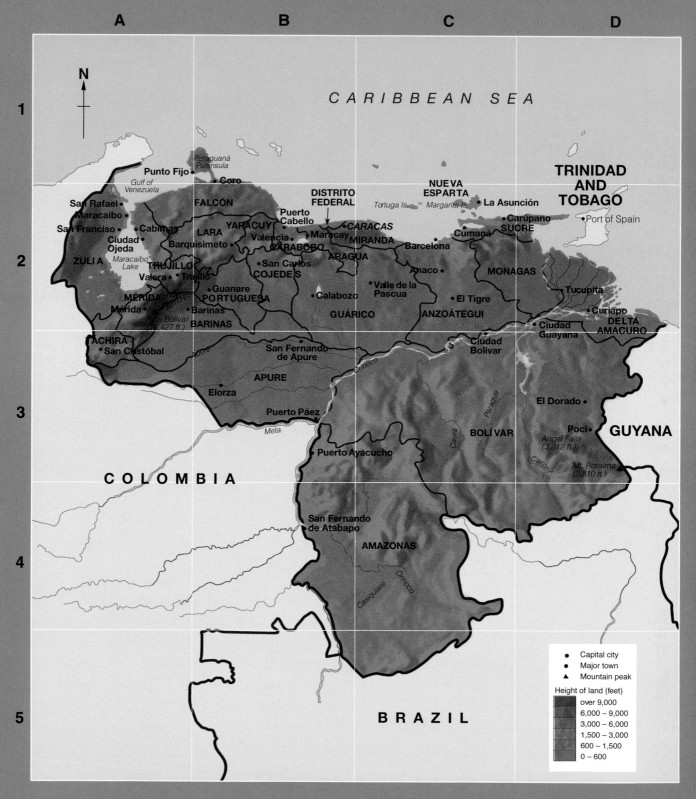

CARIBBEAN SEA

N

A

- Punto Fijo
- Coro
- Paraguaná Peninsula
- Gulf of Venezuela
- San Rafael
- Maracaibo
- San Francisco
- Cabimas
- Ciudad Ojeda
- ZULIA
- Maracaibo Lake
- TRUJILLO
- Valera
- Trujillo
- MÉRIDA
- Mérida
- Pico Bolívar (16,427 ft.)
- BARINAS
- Barinas
- TÁCHIRA
- San Cristóbal

B

- FALCÓN
- Puerto Cabello
- YARACUY
- LARA
- Barquisimeto
- Valencia
- CARABOBO
- San Carlos
- COJEDES
- Guanare
- PORTUGUESA
- DISTRITO FEDERAL
- Maracay
- San Fernando de Apure
- APURE
- Elorza
- Puerto Páez
- Meta
- Puerto Ayacucho
- San Fernando de Atabapo
- AMAZONAS
- Casiquiare

C

- NUEVA ESPARTA
- Tortuga Is.
- Margarita Is.
- La Asunción
- CARACAS
- MIRANDA
- Cumaná
- Barcelona
- ARAGUA
- Anaco
- Valle de la Pascua
- Calabozo
- GUÁRICO
- El Tigre
- ANZOÁTEGUI
- Ciudad Bolívar
- Orinoco
- Caura
- BOLÍVAR
- Paragua
- Angel Falls (3,212 ft.)
- Caroní
- Mt. Roraima (9,810 ft.)
- Orinoco

D

- TRINIDAD AND TOBAGO
- Port of Spain
- Carúpano
- SUCRE
- MONAGAS
- Tucupita
- Curiapo
- DELTA AMACURO
- Ciudad Guayana
- El Dorado
- Poci
- GUYANA

COLOMBIA

BRAZIL

Legend

- ● Capital city
- • Major town
- ▲ Mountain peak

Height of land (feet)
- over 9,000
- 6,000 – 9,000
- 3,000 – 6,000
- 1,500 – 3,000
- 600 – 1,500
- 0 – 600

MAP OF VENEZUELA

ECONOMIC VENEZUELA

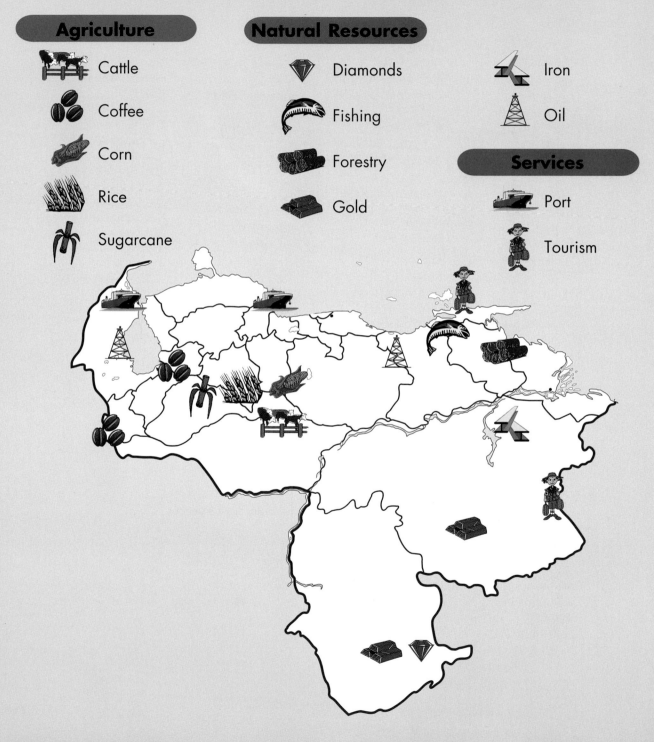

Agriculture
- Cattle
- Coffee
- Corn
- Rice
- Sugarcane

Natural Resources
- Diamonds
- Fishing
- Forestry
- Gold
- Iron
- Oil

Services
- Port
- Tourism

ABOUT THE ECONOMY

OVERVIEW
Petroleum dominates the Venezuelan economy, accounting for more than 30 percent of the GDP and around 95 percent of export earnings.

INDUSTRIES
Petroleum, construction materials, iron-ore mining, food processing, textiles, aluminum, steel, and motor vehicle assembly

GROSS DOMESTIC PRODUCT (GDP)
$345.2 billion (2010 estimate)

GDP PER CAPITA
$12,600 (2010 estimate)

GDP COMPOSITION
Industry 35 percent, services 61 percent, and agriculture 4 percent (2010 estimate)

GDP GROWTH
-1.9 percent (2010 estimate)

EXTERNAL DEBT
$55.6 billion (2010 estimate)

CURRENCY
1 Bolivar (Bs) = 100 centimos
Bs 4.3039 = $1 (2010 estimate)

INFLATION RATE
29.8 percent (2010 estimate)

AGRICULTURAL PRODUCTS
Corn, sorghum, sugarcane, rice, coffee, bananas, vegetables, beef, pork, milk

MAIN EXPORTS
Petroleum, bauxite, aluminum, minerals, chemicals, agricultural products, and basic manufactures

MAIN EXPORT PARTNERS
United States, China, Singapore, and Cuba

MAIN IMPORTS
Raw materials, agricultural products, machinery and equipment, transportation equipment, and construction materials

MAIN IMPORT PARTNERS
United States, Colombia, China, and Brazil

LABOR FORCE
13.3 million (2010 estimate)

LABOR FORCE BY OCCUPATION
Services 64 percent, agriculture 23 percent, and industry 13 percent

UNEMPLOYMENT RATE
8.5 percent (2010 estimate)

POPULATION BELOW POVERTY LINE
37.9 percent (2005 estimate)

CULTURAL VENEZUELA

La Zona Colonial de Coro
Coro's colonial center was declared a national monument in 1950. Its cobblestone streets and old colonial houses reflect the eminent role of the Spanish in Venezuela's history.

Garden City
Tree-filled Maracay is the "garden city of Venezuela." It also boasts a 7,000-seat bull ring and entry to the Henri Pittier National Park, 1,078 acres (266,380 hectares) of reserved land hosting some 550 bird species among other wildlife.

Colonia Tovar
Venezuela's gem of Germany is a little mountain town near the capital. Founded in 1843 as a settlement of German immigrants, Colonia Tovar is now a tourist spot offering Venezuelan and international visitors alike a glimpse of German culture.

Devil dance
This ceremony takes place in San Franscisco de Yare every Corpus Christi. Dancers put on papier-mache masks and red costumes and dance through the streets to the rhythm of drums and chants to scare off the devil.

Water sports
Tourists visit Margarita Island for snorkeling or scuba diving or just to lie on the sands of El Agua, the island's best beach. Other attractions include lagoons, cranes, three national parks, and the nearby fishing village of Pampatar, with its small colonial fort and colorful old buildings.

Puerto La Cruz
Beautiful beaches, access to the Mochima National Park, and boats to Margarita Island and other neighboring islands are some of the major attractions of Barcelona.

Castillo de San Antonio
South America's oldest Spanish castle, the San Antonio castle, was restored after an earthquake in 1929. It now offers visitors a panoramic view of Cumaná's cobblestone streets, castles, fortresses, and museums.

Canaima National Park
Canaima, meaning "God of Thunder," is 7.4 million acres (3 million hectares) of jungle containing the Gran Sabana and the world's highest waterfall, Angel Falls, which plunges 3,210 feet (980 m) from the Auyan Tepui, or "Devil Mountain."

Puerto Ayacucho
This tropical rain forest settlement was a camp set up in 1924 for workers building the highway to Samariapo which skirts the Orinoco upstream of Ayacucho. Indigenous Indians now come here to sell their handicrafts to tourists.

La Virgen de la Paz
A statue of the Virgin of Peace 153.2 feet (46.7 m) tall and weighing 2,000 pounds (907 kg) looks over the city of Trujillo from a mile above (1.6 km). Visitors can climb inside the monument to reach one of four points from which to see the city.

Bolivar Museum
Formerly the house where the country's first newspaper was published, now a museum exhibiting contemporary Venezuelan artworks as well as pre-Columbian art and some petroglyphs.

Jesús Soto Contemporary Art Museum
This museum in Ciudad Bolívar has eight rooms and several inner gardens exhibiting works by more than 130 artists from around the world, in particular the groundbreaking creations of Venezuelan kinetic artist Jesús Soto.

Mount Roraima
For nearly half a century, explorers could not find a way up this mile-high (1.6-km-high) sandstone plateau. Today, a single trail amid ancient forests and waterfalls leads hikers to the summit.

ABOUT THE CULTURE

OFFICIAL NAME
Bolivarian Republic of Venezuela

FLAG DESCRIPTION
A red band at the bottom and a yellow band at the top sandwich a blue band containing an arc of seven white stars.

NATIONAL ANTHEM
"Glorio al Bravo Pueblo que el Yugo Lanzo," or "Glory to the Brave Nation That Shook off the Yoke"

CLIMATE
Tropical; hot, humid; more moderate in highlands

POPULATION
27,635,743 (2011 estimate)

AGE STRUCTURE
14 years and below: 29.5 percent
15 to 64 years: 65 percent
65 years and above: 5.5 percent

LIFE EXPECTANCY
Total population: 74 years
Men: 71 years; women: 77 years (2010 estimate)

ETHNIC GROUPS
Spanish, Italian, Portuguese, Arab, German, African, and indigenous

MAIN RELIGIONS
Roman Catholic 96 percent, Protestant 2 percent, others 2 percent

MAJOR LANGUAGES
Spanish (official), numerous indigenous dialects

LITERACY
93 percent of population aged 15 years and above

NATIONAL HOLIDAYS
Declaration of Independence—April 19
Battle of Carabobo—June 24
Independence Day—July 5
Simón Bolívar's Birthday—July 24
Columbus Day—October 12
Death of Simón Bolívar—December 17

LEADERS IN POLITICS
Simón Bolívar (1783—1830)—Revolutionary leader in the fight for independence
Rómulo Betancourt (1908—81)—Leader of Acción Democrática and president 1945—48, 1959—64
Hugo Chávez Frías—President since 1998

TIME LINE

IN VENEZUELA	IN THE WORLD
5000–1500 B.C. Mesoindian cultures **1000–1500 B.C.** Neo-Indian cultures **1500 B.C.** Indo-Hispanic cultures	
	116–17 B.C. Roman Empire reaches its greatest extent, under Emperor Trajan (98–17 B.C.). **A.D. 600** Height of Mayan civilization
1498 Columbus lands on the Paria Peninsula and sees "the most beautiful lands in the world."	
1515 Cumaná, Venezuela's first colonial city, is founded.	
1527 (Santa Ana de) Coro, an important city in Venezuela's early history, is founded.	**1530** Beginning of transatlantic slave trade organized by Portuguese in Africa
1806 Francisco de Miranda twice tries unsuccessfully to liberate Venezuela from Spanish rule.	**1776** U.S. Declaration of Independence
1811 The first national congress is formed and issues a Declaration of Independence; the first constitution is established.	**1789–99** The French Revolution
1812 The First Republic falls as Monteverde takes Caracas for Spain.	
1813 Simón Bolívar establishes the Second Republic and is proclaimed Liberator.	
1814 *Llanero* leader José Tomás Boves captures Caracas, ending the Second Republic and re-establishing Spanish rule.	
1819 Bolívar is proclaimed provisional president by a second congress; a second constitution is drafted.	
1821 The Battle of Carabobo; Bolívar forms Gran Colombia.	
1829 Venezuela leaves Gran Colombia.	

IN VENEZUELA	IN THE WORLD

1835
Dr. José María Vargas becomes Venezuela's first civilian president.

1861
U.S. Civil War begins.

1878
The Bolívar becomes the currency; the national anthem is written.

1869
The Suez Canal is opened.

1908
Juan Vicente Gómez begins his dictatorship.

1914
World War I begins.

1935
Eleazar López Contreras becomes president and eventually restores some of the democracy lost under Gómez.

1939
World War II begins.

1949
North Atlantic Treaty Organization (NATO) formed

1973
Carlos Andrés Pérez becomes president on a promise to tackle privilege and poverty issues. Venezuela becomes wealthy on an oil boom.

1986
Nuclear power disaster at Chernobyl in Ukraine

1991
Breakup of Soviet Union

1999
Hugo Chávez Frías comes to power; he promises to support the people and wage war against corruption; the north of Venezuela is devastated by floods and landslides.

2000
Chávez is re-elected. There is also an unsuccessful plot to assassinate Chávez.

2001
World population surpasses 6 billion; Terrorists crash planes into New York, Washington D.C., and Pennsylvania.

2002
Mass rally to protest oil reforms and to support a general strike. Chávez is taken into military custody and his resignation is announced. Chávez returns to power. Strikes in December cause national oil shortages.

2003
War in Iraq begins.

2005
Hurricane Katrina devastates the Gulf Coast of the United States.

2006
Chávez is re-elected for another four-year term.

2007
Venezuelans vote in a referendum against extending the pace and size of Chávez's reforms.

2009
Venezuelans vote to abolish term limits, allowing Chávez to run for re-election again in 2012.

2009
Outbreak of flu virus H1N1 around the world

2010
Disastrous floods occur. The "Homeless" settle on "unoccupied land."

2011
Twin earthquake and tsunami disasters strike northeast Japan, leaving over 14,000 dead and thousands more missing.

GLOSSARY

abrazo (ah-BRAH-soh)
An embrace between Venezuelans when they meet.

caraqueño (kah-rah-KAIR-nyoh)
A resident of Caracas.

comadre (kom-MAH-dray)
Godmother.

compadre (kom-PAH-dray)
Godfather.

criollo
A Creole. The term originally referred to a person of Spanish ancestry; now it describes anyone or anything indigenous to Venezuela.

cuatro (KWAH-troh)
A small guitar with four strings.

hacienda
A large plantation or estate.

hamaca (ah-MAH-kah)
A tightly woven hammock.

llanero (yah-NAIR-roh)
Someone who dwells in the llanos, usually a cowboy.

llanos
The vast central plains of Venezuela.

manta
An intricately woven shawl worn by Spanish and Latin American women.

mestizo
Originally referred to a person of mixed Spanish-Indian ancestry; now describes anyone of mixed ethnicity.

piñata
Bright-colored figure filled with candy and toys; it is hit with a stick at children's birthday parties until it releases its contents.

quinceañera (kin-seh-ah-nih-AIR-rah)
A girl's 15th birthday.

rancho
A makeshift home built on the outskirts of large cities, especially around Caracas.

tepui (tair-POO-ee)
A flat-topped rock formation in the Guiana Highlands.

Venezolano (beh-neh-zoh-LAH-noh)
A Venezuelan.

⟫ FOR FURTHER INFORMATION

BOOKS

Dinneen, Mark. *Culture and Customs of Venezuela (Culture and Customs of Latin America and the Caribbean).* Santa Barbara, CA: Greenwood Publishing Group, 2008.

Maddicks, Russell. *Venezuela (The Bradt Travel Guide).* Bucks, England, UK: Bradt Travel Guides, 2011.

Nichols, Elizabeth Gackstetter and Kimberly J. Morse. *Venezuela (Latin America in Focus).* Santa Barbara, CA: ABC-CLIO, 2010.

Tarver, H. Michael and Julia C. Frederick. *The History of Venezuela (Palgrave Essential Histories).* Hampshire, UK: Palgrave Macmillan, 2006.

Wilpert, Gregory. *Changing Venezuela by Taking Power: The History and Policies of the Chavez Government.* Brooklyn, NY: Verso Books, 2006.

MUSIC

Folk Music from Venezuela. United Kingdom: Arc, 2000.

WEBSITES

About the Auyantepui in the Roraima group of mountains. Includes a slide show. www.mother.com/-cwitham/tepui.html#angelfalls

Country study of Venezuela. www.lcweb2.loc.gov/frd/cs/vetoc.html

Country Studies—Venezuela. http://lcweb2.loc.gov/frd/cs/vetoc.html

Embassy of Venezuela in the United States. www.embavenez-us.org/

History of the Bolívar Peninsula and the life of Simón Bolívar. www.crystalbeach.com/history.htm

Photos of and facts on the spectacled bear. http://scz.org/animals/b/spbear.html

Virtual tour of Venezuela. www.orinoco.org/

BIBLIOGRAPHY

BOOKS

Boehm, Lincoln A. *Venezuela in Pictures. Visual Geography series.* Minneapolis: Lerner Publications Company, 1998.

Boulais, Sue. *Andres Galarraga: A Real-Life Reader Biography.* Elkton, Germany: Mitchell Lane Publishers, 1998.

Country Report: *Venezuela.* London: Economist Intelligence Unit, 1993.

George, Jean Craighead. *One Day in the Tropical Rain Forest.* New York: Ty Crowell Company, 1990.

Heinrichs, Ann. *Venezuela.* San Francisco: Children's Press, 1994.

Horenstein, Henry. *Baseball in the Barrios.* San Diego: Gulliver Books, 1997.

Jones, Helga. *Venezuela. Globe-Trotters Club series.* Minneapolis: Carolrhoda Books, 2000.

———. *Venezuela. A Ticket To series.* Minneapolis: Carolrhoda Books, 2000.

Morrison, Marion. *Venezuela. Major World Nations series.* New York: Chelsea House Publishers, 1998.

Popic, Miro, ed. *Ecotourism Guide to Venezuela.* Caracas: Miro Popic, 2000.

Rawlins, Carol B. *The Orinoco River. Watts Library: World of Water series.* New York: Franklin Watts, 1999.

South America, Central America & the Caribbean. London: Europa Publications, 1992.

WEBSITES

BBC Country Profile—Venezuela. http://news.bbc.co.uk/2/hi/americas/country_profiles/1229345.stm

Ethnologue—Languages of Venezuela. www.ethnologue.com/show_country.asp?name=VE

Infoplease—Venezuela. www.infoplease.com/ipa/A0108140.html

Internet World Stats—Venezuela. www.internetworldstats.com/sa/ve.htm

Lonely Planet—Introducing Venezuela. www.lonelyplanet.com/venezuela

Online Newspapers—Venezuela. www.onlinenewspapers.com/venezuel.htm

The World Factbook (Central Intelligence Agency)—Venezuela. https://www.cia.gov/library/publications/the-world-factbook/geos/ve.html

Think Venezuela. www.think-venezuela.net

Travel State—Venezuela. http://travel.state.gov/travel/cis_pa_tw/cis/cis_1059.html

The Washington Post—Venezuela. www.washingtonpost.com/wp-srv/world/countries/venezuela.html

U.S. Department of State—Venezuela. www.state.gov/r/pa/ei/bgn/35766.htm

Venezuelan Analysis. http://venezuelanalysis.com/

World Health Organisation—Venezuela. www.who.int/countries/ven/en/

INDEX